Leviathan

*This book is a publication
of the Hoover Institution's*
**Initiative
on
*Accountability of
Government to Society***

Leviathan

*The Growth of
Local Government
and the
Erosion of Liberty*

Clint Bolick

HOOVER INSTITUTION PRESS
Stanford University Stanford, California

www.hoover.org

Hoover Institution Press Publication No. 531

First printing 2004
10 09 08 07 06 05 04   9 8 7 6 5 4 3 2 1

Manufactured in the United States of America
The paper used in this publication meets the minimum requirements
of American National Standard for Information Sciences — Permanence
of Paper for Printed Library Materials, ANSI Z39.48-1992. ♾

Library of Congress Cataloging-in-Publication Data
Bolick, Clint.
   Leviathan : the growth of local government and the erosion of liberty /
by Clint Bolick.
        p.   cm. — (Hoover Institution Press publication ; no. 531)
      Includes bibliographical references and index.
      ISBN 0-8179-4552-0 (alk. paper)
      1. Local government — United States.   2. Civil rights — United States.
I. Title.   II. Series: Hoover Institution Press publication ; 531.
JS331B65   2004
320.8′0973 — dc22   2004004401

For my son,
Ryne Austin Bolick

CONTENTS

ACKNOWLEDGMENTS

I am honored that this book is a collaboration with the Hoover Institution, which has emerged as one of the most creative, thoughtful, and influential public-policy organizations in America. I am especially indebted to John Raisian, Patricia Baker, Richard Sousa, and Ann Wood for their support of this project.

This book builds upon my previous work, *Grassroots Tyranny and the Limits of Federalism*, which was published a decade ago by the Cato Institute. I am grateful to Cato for allowing me to develop the themes and concepts upon which I build here.

While I was writing this book, I served as vice president

and national director of state chapters for the Institute for Justice, the nation's premier pro-freedom public-interest law firm, which I cofounded in 1991 with Chip Mellor. Many of the stories set forth in this book derive from cases litigated by IJ. As this book was headed to publication, I joined a new organization, the Alliance for School Choice, as its president and general counsel, to address education reform issues discussed in chapter 9. I remain affiliated with IJ as its strategic litigation counsel. I hope this book will serve as a fitting tribute to my more than twelve years at IJ and to my colleagues there, who serve as a constant source of inspiration and optimism.

Finally, I give thanks to those many (yet all too few) individuals who make possible the kind of freedom activism put into theory and practice by such groups as the Hoover Institution, the Institute for Justice, and the Alliance for School Choice. Were it not for your tangible commitment, we could not win the battle of ideas and extend freedom to those in our nation who lack it. With your support, we have only begun to fight.

Clint Bolick
Phoenix, Arizona
February 2004

INTRODUCTION

Pop quiz. Name the president of the United States.

Got it? That was easy.

How about your two United States senators? Your member of the House of Representatives? Bravo if you're still scoring 100 percent.

Now they get trickier. Name your mayor. Name a member of the school board. Not all of them—just one.

Give up yet? How about a member of the county governing board? The local planning commission? The local zoning board? The special authority that delivers your water?

Anyone picking up this book is probably better informed than the average person. Yet can even the most sophisticated reader answer all of those questions? (I'm the author, and I was stumped after the fourth question.) We all know who our national elected officials are, but as they get closer to home, the image gets a bit fuzzier. It is a sad commentary on the state of our representative democracy that a majority of Americans probably don't know who their two U.S. senators are. When it comes to local officials like county board members and planning commissioners, the vast majority of people probably don't even know they exist, much less their identities.

And yet, it is not as if those individuals are unimportant. To the contrary, on essential matters of vital importance to every American—the quality of our children's schools; the capabilities of police and fire departments; the provision of water, electricity, and sewage services; the amount of sales and property taxes—those local officials whose names and faces we don't even know are far more consequential to the intimate aspects of our everyday lives than the president.

Indeed, our nation was designed that it be so. Initially, we were a confederation of state governments that bound together for common but limited national purposes. From that initial experiment, we created a constitution intended to create a national government of limited and defined powers while keeping most government close to home where we could keep an eye on it.

Things haven't worked out exactly as planned with regard to the first of those two constitutional objectives. We have a huge national government whose power is largely unchecked. Indeed, when most Americans think of "big government," surely the image they conjure is our massive, remote, avaricious national capital.

In reality, the national government has downsized somewhat since the Reagan era. But President Bill Clinton had it wrong when he declared that the era of big government was over.

It just moved to the suburbs.

In a perverse sense, Americans have achieved their objective of primarily local government: The combined bulk of state and local government now exceeds that of the entire federal government—even including the military—in both size and spending. Furthermore, even as the national government shrinks or stays relatively stable in size, state and local governments are growing—in size, number, wealth, and power. And while they may be close to home, most Americans are decidedly *not* keeping an eye on them. Though we care deeply about who our president is, most of us could not care less about the nameless, faceless officials who run our local governments.

That is a big mistake. While the national government has the power to infringe upon the rights of Americans—and does so frequently, and often with impunity—state and local governments often pose an even greater threat, both because their actions touch more intimately the everyday lives of ordinary Americans, and because of their very invisibility. If the president starts an unpopular war or raises taxes, people know who to blame and they direct their energy accordingly. But if your kid gets a lousy education in public school, or your local government decides to exercise eminent domain to take your home or business, it is often impossible even to find out who is responsible, much less how to fight it. Someone figured all that out long ago when coining the adage, "You can't fight city hall."

Fortunately, you can—but it's rarely easy, and never painless. Supposedly, in our federalist system we revere local government because we can better control it. But too often the rules are rigged in favor of government—and particularly local government. Ordinary Americans are usually no match for special-interest groups whose sole purpose is to manipulate the power of government for their own benefit. Courts are reluctant to disturb local government prerogatives except in the most extraordinary circumstances—even if the government officials involved are democratically unaccountable. Fighting local government can be like banging your head against a wall.

My colleagues and I at the Institute for Justice sue bureaucrats for a living. Representing David against the governmental Goliath, we provide the legal slingshot. We find that when someone's rights are infringed by government, it usually takes place at the hands of some state or local government official. One of the purposes of this book is to share our experiences, both to illustrate the grave threat that state and local governments pose to liberty, and to demonstrate that it is possible to fight back.

My own interest in what I have come to call grassroots tyranny stems from two episodes earlier in my life. The first occurred when I was a teenager in Linden, New Jersey, a suburb of New York City. Linden was (and decades later, still is) dominated by a corrupt, venal Democratic political machine that controlled every facet of political life in the city, from taxes to contracts to abundant patronage. At its helm was the autocratic mayor, John T. Gregorio.

Growing up with an interest in politics, and displaying an affinity for the underdog that continues to this day, I aligned myself with the sole Republican on the 11-member city council, a retired insurance executive named Joseph P. Locascio. The avuncular Locascio became not only my political mentor but almost a surrogate dad, vowing to me with a grin, "I'll make a Sicilian out of you yet." He taught me to value principle and integrity above partisanship and political power, quipping, "if you vote for the donkey or the elephant, that's what you get."

Well ahead of his time in the 1970s, Locascio championed such populist reforms as an elected board of education and term limits for elected officials. The machine did not pay much heed to Locascio's often quixotic efforts—until he succeeded in enacting, through a voter initiative, an elected school board, thereby depriving the machine of a huge source of patronage.

As it always does, the empire struck back, engaging in a savage personal smear campaign that nearly ruined Locascio's reputation in Linden. I watched in horror as a man I respected beyond any other was laid low by vicious bullies for whom the ends justified the means. Valuing his good name and family over his political career, Locascio resigned and moved out of town, removing the only political thorn from the side of the machine.

Subsequently, Mayor Gregorio was convicted of various acts of corruption, stripped of his political offices (he also served as a state senator), and sentenced to jail. But politics in New Jersey transcends partisan lines, and a Republican governor, Thomas Kean, pardoned Gregorio, who was once again elected mayor of Linden, where he presides to this day.*

While in law school at the University of California at Davis, I encountered grassroots tyranny of a different sort. The city of Davis, like many other college towns, leans politically to the fringe left. In the early 1980s, left-wing activists led by Jane Fonda and Tom Hayden created an organization called the Campaign for Economic Democracy (CED), whose mission was to effectuate a redistribution of society's wealth.

---

*In college, I wrote my political science honors thesis about Linden's political machine. I attended Drew University, whose current president is none other than the same Tom Kean who pardoned Gregorio.

The method they chose to achieve that goal was not national politics, but *local* politics, a strategy built upon two critical insights: (1) that it is easier to dominate local rather than national politics; and (2) that local government has the greatest control over society's wealth.

CED set out to seize power in local governments, and they did just that in cities such as Berkeley, Santa Monica, and Davis. Then came the agenda: rent control, regulations on the use of property, campaign contribution and spending limits, minimum-wage increases, antispeculation ordinances, and the like. College towns in California became little socialist utopias, and so they largely remain to this day.

Fortunately, while in law school I also took a course in local government, and learned that there are two powerful weapons for combating grassroots tyranny. The first is the 14th Amendment to the U.S. Constitution, which guarantees the privileges or immunities of citizenship, equal protection, and due process. The second is a wonderful federal statute that ought to have a respectful name but only has a number: 42 U.S.C. § 1983. This law allows private individuals to sue state or local government officials who violate federal constitutional rights while acting "under color of state law." (Happily, under another provision, successful litigants can collect attorney fees, too.) As I studied all of this, the lightbulbs started switching on. In § 1983, I saw the path to a very rewarding (if not particularly remunerative) legal career.

"Wait a minute," you might ask, "how can a self-professed libertarian champion the invocation of national power against innocent and defenseless local governments? Doesn't that violate the basic precepts of federalism?"

Good question, and one that vexed me for a long time, until I began investigating what federalism was all about. Like most people, I reflexively thought of federalism as synonymous with "states' rights." So to use national power in a way that trenched upon state sovereignty must conflict with federalism.

Not exactly, it turns out. The framers were deeply concerned about the expansion of national power, and they created a number of mechanisms (among them federalism) to prevent this expansion. But they also keenly understood the tendency of local governments to abuse individual rights. Indeed, the propensity of states to enact protectionist trade barriers was one of the greatest motivations for replacing the Articles of Confederation and creating a stronger national government in the first place. A fundamental purpose of the Constitution was to provide a check against state governments that indulged parochial interests above individual liberty and the general welfare.

Still, the framers believed that between the two governments, the states would be the more reliable guardians of individual liberty. Federalism was seen not as a means of protecting state sovereignty as an end in itself, but as a means of achieving the greater end of safeguarding individual liberty. As a result, the original constitution narrowly defined the powers of the national government, while the Tenth Amendment reserved to the states all residual governmental powers.

Over time, however, the premise underlying that system — that states were the more reliable guardians of liberty — proved incorrect, particularly when, acting under the mantle of states' rights, they sought to preserve the greatest nullification of individual liberty, the institution of human slavery. Following the Civil War, the tapestry of federalism was reworked through the enactment of the 14th Amendment, which guaranteed against state abuse the privileges or immunities of citizens, equal protection under the law, and due process of law. The 14th Amendment, when conjoined with other provisions of the Constitution that preserved state autonomy, created a mutual balance of power between the states and the national government, aimed at protecting individual liberty.

Ultimately, a balanced and comprehensive examination of the American concept of federalism yields an important insight: that the notion of states' rights is an oxymoron. States do not have rights. States have powers. People have rights. And the purpose of federalism is to ensure that government at every level abides those rights.

I first wrote about this topic a decade ago in a book published by the Cato Institute called *Grassroots Tyranny: The Limits of Federalism*.[1] By that time, I had been practicing law at the Institute for Justice for two years, and had already witnessed (and challenged) a number of abuses of state and local government power. Over the years, I have heard from a number of people who have read *Grassroots Tyranny*. The common thread binding all of these readers together is that each one, whether liberal or conservative, has found within it at least *some* example of grassroots tyranny that strikes personally close to home. It is from that convergence of experience that I hope will flow greater concern, among both liberals and conservatives, about the scope and abuse of government power in our own backyards.

In this book, I revisit *Grassroots Tyranny* from the vantage point of two decades in the litigation trenches.* If anything, my initial concerns have grown. Local government is at once more voracious, far-reaching, and recklessly deployed than I ever realized. And increasingly it is wielded by officials and

---

*Prior to cofounding the Institute for Justice in 1991, I challenged abuses of local government power at the Mountain States Legal Foundation; the U.S. Department of Justice, Civil Rights Division; and the Landmark Legal Foundation Center for Civil Rights.

entities that are virtually invisible to most of the public. It is the experiences of ordinary Americans locked in combat with their local governments—and the insights that my colleagues and I have gained from those experiences—that provide the bulk of this book.

My colleagues and I have litigated most of the cases discussed in chapters 4–6, mostly successfully, sometimes not. Some that we lost in court, we won in the court of public opinion. Local government often commits its misdeeds under cover of public darkness; but like the demons of folklore, it doesn't stand up well to the light of day.

I think I can make one prediction safely: Almost everyone reading this book will find that some of the stories of grassroots tyranny infuriate them, while others make them want to stand up and cheer. To counter that instinct, I use the first two chapters to set the stage by discussing the principles underlying our constitutional system of federalism, and by making a plea for consistent application of those principles. Grassroots tyranny finds fertile soil in the uneven application of the rules designed to protect our freedom. Even if we sometimes are offended by the way some people exercise their freedom, we must scrupulously protect their freedom if we are to have any prospect of protecting it for ourselves.

Since writing *Grassroots Tyranny*, I have developed a greater appreciation for the tools that are available to combat infringements of liberty by state and local governments. So in addition to raising an alarm, I hope to provide a fairly optimistic assessment of the prospects for retethering local governments to their proper bounds of power. I hope that you will find the pages to follow illuminating and useful—and worth doing something about.

PART ONE

The Nature of the Beast

1

Leviathan

CLOSE YOUR EYES and ponder for a moment the American ideal of local government. The image, no doubt, is a bucolic one. Invariably it revolves around a town hall, filled with informed, civic-minded citizens expressing their views and reaching consensus. Public-spirited officials manage the town's affairs. A sheriff, maybe named Andy, maintains order and provides a friendly jail cell where the local town drunk can sleep it off, while the fire department rescues wayward cats from trees. The townspeople turn out on holidays for parades down Main Street. The city is tidy, streets are cleaned, garbage is collected. Around election time the town has good-natured debates and spirited political rallies. The schools have strong parent/teacher associations and citizens serve on blue-ribbon committees to sort through problems. You can almost smell the apple pies cooling on the windowsills.

If television shows are any gauge, this was the common image that Americans held of their towns as late as the 1960s. Little wonder that many Americans, especially conservatives, harbor almost nostalgic views about local government, and hold the principle of "local autonomy" as a matter of fervent faith. This attachment to localism has grown over time. In 1936, when Americans were asked if they preferred a concentration of power in the national or the state governments, 56 percent favored the national government, with only 44 percent preferring the states. By 1995, only 26 percent favored the national government, while 64 percent preferred the states (and 10 percent were not sure).[1] Americans like their government close to home, the old-fashioned way.

Now open your eyes and look at your city government. Andy and his pals have been replaced by an army of nameless, faceless bureaucrats. Government has proliferated to the point that you don't even know how many governments regulate you, much less their identities. Widespread corruption leads government officials to resign and march off to jail. Taxes are sky-high. Turnout in municipal elections is appallingly low; turnout in bond elections and school board races lower still. The city requires permits and charges fees for everything. Public employees are constantly demanding wage increases and going on strike. An inverse correlation exists between the local government functions you *wish* were efficiently administered (e.g., snow removal and schools) and those that *are* efficiently administered (e.g., parking meter enforcement).*

---

*Back in my days working in the District of Columbia, I used to advise

Welcome to America in the 21st century, in which the most significant (yet almost entirely unremarked-upon) phenomenon in our political system is the explosive growth of local government, both in absolute terms and relative to the national government. It proves the old adage "be careful what you wish for because you might just get it": Americans want government close to home, and boy, do they have it.

And not always benevolent governments, either. Local governments are often malign, if for no other reason than the propensity of people with power to abuse it. The effect can be dramatic, for local government touches our lives in direct and intimate ways. As historian James McGregor Burns puts it, "Local government is not only a very big deal; it is costly and overlapping, and it affects nearly every one of us every day."[2] He explains, "State and local governments deal more directly with the average person than the national government does, because neighborhood, school, and housing problems are closely regulated by state and local governments."[3] From schools to police protection to water to streets to trash collection to the houses we can build and the businesses we can operate, local government controls it all. Cities today not only provide basic services but are engaged in all manner of activities never contemplated by the framers, from providing welfare and government housing to constructing and operating sports arenas and water parks. Local government is not just big government, it is big business.

Local governments possess enormous power to redistribute wealth and opportunities, impacting in real and tangible ways the real lives of real people. Examples are legion (and fill

---

visitors that if they happened to suffer the misfortune of being victims of a crime, they should try to do it near an expired parking meter, because the police response time is much quicker.

much of this book). As one political scientist notes, for instance, "By means of their decisions regarding zoning and the use of land, suburbanites have often been able to keep racial minorities, poor people, and tenants penned up in the central city."[4] Similarly (though political machines are often thought to have gone the way of the dinosaurs), patronage remains a way of life. A study of capital improvement allocations that were made by the administration of Denver mayor Federico Peña during the 1980s, for example, found that neighborhoods' receipt of outlays correlated closely with their ethnic makeups and the amount of political support they'd given the mayor in the most recent elections. Identifiably white neighborhoods that opposed Peña had 12 percent of the city's population but received 7 percent of capital outlays, Hispanic neighborhoods accounted for 5 percent of the population and 28 percent of the city's capital expenditures, and identifiably black neighborhoods accounted for 7 percent of the population but received only 2 percent of the outlays.[5]

At the same time, corrupt or arbitrary public officials can punish opponents in subtle ways, such as by denying or delaying the myriad permits needed to develop property or to operate businesses. Local governments are particularly susceptible to the influence of special interests, for as Burns explains, "group interests can be concentrated in states and localities, whereas their strength tends to be diluted in the national government."[6] It all amounts to a system in which the government that is closest to home can be very alien and hostile to average constituents who just want to be left alone.

We are all at the mercy of local governments. And they are everywhere.

Big Government: At a Location Near You

Revealing a penchant for understatement, political scientist Virginia Perrenod observes that "Americans have a propensity for multiple governments."[7] The Chicago metropolitan area alone is regulated by more than 1,200 different governmental jurisdictions;* the Philadelphia metropolitan area by 864 governmental units; the Pittsburgh area by 744.[8] Overall in 1997 there were 87,453 local governments in the United States, an increase from 78,218 in 1972, 25 years earlier.[9] At that rate, an average of *one new local government is created in America every single day.*

State and local governments spend voraciously. As of 1999, state and local governments were expending 1.06 trillion dollars annually, accounting for 11.5 percent of the nation's gross domestic product. As figure 1 illustrates, state and local spending eclipsed combined federal government spending around 1970, and the trajectory continues as state and local governments make up an ever-increasing proportion of overall American government.

These figures likely understate the growing gap between federal spending and spending by state and local governments, as they don't reveal the massive amount of federal moneys distributed as aid to state and local governments. In 1970, federal aid to state and local governments totaled 24 billion dollars, accounting for 2.4 percent of the gross domestic product. By 2000, that amount had increased to 284 billion dollars, or a full 3 percent of the gross domestic product.[10]

State spending has soared over the past five decades. As

*For that reason in part, the Institute for Justice in 1998 opened its Clinic on Entrepreneurship at the University of Chicago Law School. The clinic assists aspiring low-income entrepreneurs through the regulatory maze they must navigate in order to create legitimate business enterprises.

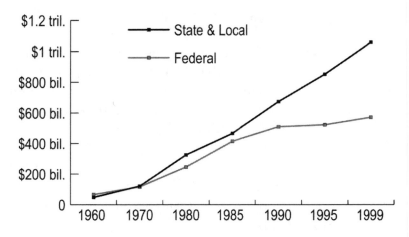

Figure 1   Relative Expenditures and Growth by Level of
Government
Source: U.S. Census Bureau, *Statistical Abstract of the United States* (2000),
p. 451.

figure 2 demonstrates, state per capita spending, measured in
constant 1996 dollars, has more than quadrupled since 1961,
growing from $638 in 1961 to $2,983 in 2001.[11] Viewed in
terms of spending, the size of state government relative to
population has increased by roughly one-third over each of
the past two decades.

Although federal grants account for 31.4 percent of state
and local revenues,[12] state and local governments derive the
vast majority of revenues from taxes and fees. Altogether,
state and local governments collect more than $872 billion in
taxes.[13] On average, in 1996 states taxed at a rate of $1,759 per
capita—with Connecticut collecting the highest taxes, at
$2,870 per capita.[14] Cities add hefty taxes, especially through
property assessments. In 1996, New York City alone collected
more than $18 billion in taxes.[15] State and local debt also
climbed during the 1990s, from $861 billion in 1990 to $1.17

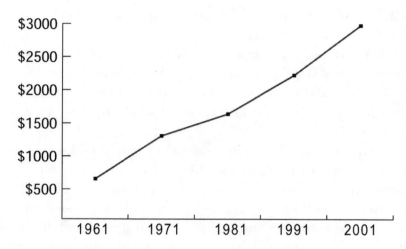

Figure 2   Growth of Per Capita State Spending (constant 1996 dollars)

Source: John Maggs, "Sorry States," *National Journal* (Aug. 9, 2003), p. 2537.

trillion in 1996—an increase from $3,459 to $4,412 in debt per capita.[16]

Many states are facing huge budget deficits, necessitating increased taxes or reduced services. The disappearing act that transformed massive budget surpluses into deficits would make even the most talented magician shake his head in wonder. In 1998, the states had amassed budget surpluses totaling nearly $60 billion. By the first quarter of 2003, the surpluses had turned into a collective deficit of nearly $65 billion. California alone racked up $38 billion in debt. The states' deficits were so gaping that, by late 2003, they were exerting a serious drag on economic recovery. Many states were forced to cut spending, particularly among aid programs for the poor; this in turn reduced consumer spending.[17] The situation is so dire that analyst Gregg Easterbrook concludes that "state deficits

will be among the country's leading domestic political issues
for the next several years."[18]

Many states have turned to massive tax hikes, which also
dampen jobs and economic growth. States raised taxes $6.9
billion in 2003, following even larger tax increases totaling
$9.1 billion in 2002, the largest one-year hike in state taxes in
more than a decade.[19]

State officials blamed the recession for their budget problems, but the real culprit was their own voracious spending
during days of economic plenty. An analysis by *USA Today*
found that the fiscal woes of most states are the consequence
not of a weakened economy but of fiscal irresponsibility by
the states themselves, who continued to increase spending
(up 6.3 percent in the fiscal year that ended on June 30, 2002)
even as revenues declined. While the private sector registered
a net loss of 2.6 million jobs between 2001 and 2003, state governments added 74,000 jobs. All states except Vermont have
balanced-budget laws, but many use accounting gimmicks to
skirt the requirements. The worst offender is California,
which spends one billion dollars more each month than it
takes in. The *USA Today* analysis found that Utah is the most
fiscally responsible state, while California, Montana, Mississippi, West Virginia, Tennessee, Rhode Island, Oklahoma,
Illinois, Colorado, and Arizona are the least responsible.[20]

Another scapegoat the states attribute their maladies to is
the federal government: Why doesn't it just send them more
money? The trouble with that solution, says Gregg Easterbrook, is that it "presents a problem of its own: To bail out the
states, the federal government would have to obtain money
from taxpayers. Taxpayers who live in—states."[21] It's a costly
shell game. "Ever since World War II, the nation's governors
. . . have relied on a bookkeeping switcheroo in which Congress taxes Americans (that is, residents of states) at a higher

rate than the federal budget actually requires and then sends some of the revenue back to the states," explains Easterbrook. "This arrangement allows governors to denounce the big spenders in Washington while simultaneously relying on the big spenders in Washington to keep state budgets in the black."[22]

To be fair, a lot of the federal aid is earmarked to offset state spending for massive unfunded federal mandates. The better course would be to eliminate the unfunded mandates and put a halt to federal revenue sharing. The system is inherently inefficient, deploying the federal government as a middleman in the routing of funds from taxpayers to the states. That in turn lends itself to political manipulation, by which those states having more-powerful congressional delegations bring home the bacon while their neighbors go hungry. Moreover, "Voters should know what government costs," argues Easterbrook. But the current system "makes state and local governments seem cheaper than they really are."[23]

Despite gaping budget deficits, state government continues to grow. Between 1997 and 2002, state spending grew by more than 6 percent annually—more than twice the average 2.25 percent rate of inflation. Although they often accuse Democrats of being big spenders, Republicans actually are more likely to increase state spending. State legislatures controlled by Republicans increased spending by 6.54 percent each year during that period, compared to 6.17 percent in legislatures controlled by Democrats. Worst of all were states whose governor and legislature were both Republican; these increased spending at a 6.85 percent annual clip.[24]

State and local government is also larger than the national government when measured in terms of the number of people employed. Fully 86 percent of all civilian government employees now work for state and local governments. The number of

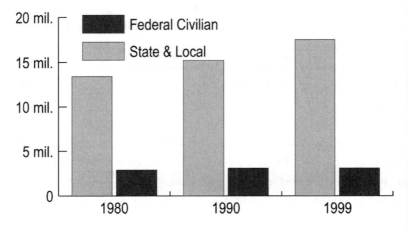

Figure 3   Relative Size of Government Workforces
Source: U.S. Census Bureau, *Statistical Abstract of the United States* (2000),
p. 430.

federal civilian employees actually shrank from 2.9 million in
1980 to fewer than 2.7 million in 1999, while the number of
state and local government employees during that same
period grew from 13.3 million to nearly 17.5 million (see figure 3). Among those, roughly three-quarters work for local
governments. State and local government employees account
for roughly 13.6 percent of the nation's total workforce.

Taking the average household size of 2.62 persons, that
means that 46 million Americans — 16 percent of the U.S.
population — are either employed by state or local government
or directly dependent on someone who is. That makes for a
fairly potent special-interest group — about which I will have
more to say at the end of this chapter.

One major difference between the private and public
workforces is the degree of unionization. While labor unions
have declined in the private sector, they flourish in the government sector (see figure 4). Fewer than 10 percent of pri-

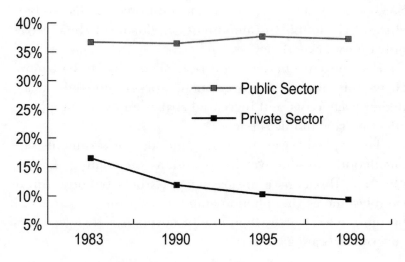

Figure 4   Relative Degree of Unionization
Source: U.S. Census Bureau, *Statistical Abstract of the United States* (2000), p. 445.

vate-sector workers are unionized, compared to more than 37 percent of government employees. In 1983, government workers constituted less than one-third of all unionized employees; by 1999, they accounted for 43 percent. The main public-sector union, the American Federation of State, County, and Municipal Employees (AFSCME), has 1.3 million members nationwide; additionally, more than half of the members of the similarly sized Service Employees International Union are employed in the public sector. That gives state and local government employees the best of all possible worlds: job security and collective bargaining.[25]

Unionization translates into higher wages for government-sector employees, who average $641 per week versus $549 for all workers.[26] Benefits often widen the gap even further. In New York City, the average city employee receives

$58,660 per year in wages, and an additional $24,062 in benefits, nearly double the amount of benefits he or she received only four years earlier.[27]

For the citizenry, by contrast, all of that is bad news. Heavy unionization of government workers not only means higher wage costs, but increased strikes and work stoppages affecting vital public services.[28]

The explosive growth of state and local governments saps our nation's productive vitality and, as the coming chapters illustrate, threatens even greater grassroots tyranny. But as troublesome as this phenomenon appears on the surface, it becomes even worse when one discovers exactly *which* local governments are growing.

Invisible Governments

One of the most powerful officials in the history of New York—one of the largest cities on earth—was named neither LaGuardia nor Giuliani. He was neither governor nor mayor, though early in his career he campaigned for the first office and was nominated for the second. In fact, the most powerful man in New York gained his might largely as a political appointee. This man, heralded in his time and now largely forgotten, was Robert Moses. He presided over the city for 34 years (1934–68) variously as its parks commissioner, construction director, and as the head of the Triborough Bridge Authority, which through his machinations evolved into the Triborough Bridge and Tunnel Authority (referred to hereafter in this text simply as "Triborough").

In those capacities, Moses built much of what we know as New York, masterminding and implementing the construction of almost every single major road and bridge; 416 miles of parkways in the suburbs; massive public works projects including Lincoln Center, the New York Coliseum, the United Nations, and the Fordham, Pratt, and Long Island University campuses; 650 parks; and 148,000 apartments.[29]

Moses was also the leading architect of the modern form of urban governance. In 1974, Robert Caro, before he began his epic multivolume biography of Lyndon Johnson, published a 1,162-page biography titled *The Power Broker: Robert Moses and the Fall of New York*. In it, Caro chronicled how the brilliant and fiercely ambitious Moses transformed a form of urban government—the "public authority"—from humble origins into a source of enormous political power, patronage, wealth, and influence, all of it outside the grasp of democratic accountability.

Moses saw that public authorities in his time possessed the autonomy of a private corporation as well as some of the powers of a government, such as the power of eminent domain, the power to regulate projects within their jurisdiction, and the power to issue bonds.[30] But they also had limits. Prior to the creation of the New York Port Authority, each public authority was established to effect only one public improvement, to issue only enough bonds to pay for it, to transfer ownership and control to the government that created the authority, and then to go out of existence.[31] Moses recognized that he could expand the power of Triborough exponentially if he could find a way to give public authorities indefinite duration and the ability both to take on multiple projects and to keep and reinvest revenues. Those vastly expanded powers, observes Caro, amounted to creating, "within a democratic system based upon a division of powers among three branches of government, a new, fourth branch, a branch that would, moreover, in significant respects, be independent of the other three."[32]

As the legislature gave Moses what he wanted, Triborough

became ubiquitous, expanding its domain far beyond the two
bridges it was initially created to build, to now encompass the
construction of roads, public works, beaches, and parks.
Reaping massive tolls from bridge and road projects, the public authority amassed enormous wealth, entering into
thousands of contracts and creating a host of grateful multi-
millionaires.[33] United by self-interest behind his schemes
were "banks, labor unions, contractors, bond underwriters,
insurance firms, the great retail stores, [and] real estate
manipulators."[34] As Caro explains, Moses "used the power of
money to undermine the democratic processes of the largest
city in the world, to plan and build its parks, bridges, high-
ways, and housing projects on the basis of his whim alone."[35]

Moses's methods in achieving his grandiose ambitions
were "dictatorial, peremptory, arbitrary, arrogant."[36] Triborough was hugely bloated and inefficient.[37] But Moses could
get away with it; indeed, he could project himself as "a fearless
independent above politics," and his reign spanned the ten-
ure of six governors and five mayors, of both parties. Like a
corporation, the public authority's records were private, and
it was not required to hold public hearings. But unlike a private corporation, it was not accountable to shareholders, or
really to anyone.[38]

This type of behemoth, runaway government that is
largely invisible to the public contributed to the greatest trag-
edy in recent American history. In the 1950s, David Rockefeller wanted to build a new headquarters for Chase Manhattan
Bank. As so many powerful businesspeople do, Rockefeller
turned not to voluntary market processes, but to the government. He enlisted Austin Tobin, the czar of the Port Authority, whose power rivaled if not exceeded that of Robert Moses.

In Tobin's mind, the project evolved into the colossus that
became the World Trade Center. And in his hands, it became,

in the words of a prominent New York developer, "an uncon-
querable Frankenstein."[39]

Tobin reasoned that the project was within his jurisdiction because, after all, "The Port Authority mission always
included promotion of the port."[40] He designed a project on a
scale so grandiose that it could only be rivaled by his own ego.
Rockefeller's own study by McKinsey & Co. cautioned against
the project, but Tobin pushed forward.

Mayor David Wagner had serious reservations from the
start, but even the city was powerless to stop it. Because the
Port Authority was exempt from the city's building and safety
codes, developers were able to skirt the risk of building two
110-story towers. And subsequent maintenance was not up to
code.[41]

The types of governments that Robert Moses and Austin
Tobin ran were relatively rare in their day, but have come to
be commonplace—in fact, special districts are now, by far, the
most numerous form of government in America. They form
the backbone of our nation's invisible governments. Everyone
knows that there are nameless, faceless, unelected and largely
unaccountable bureaucrats who exert tremendous control
over our lives. But mostly when we conjure an image of them,
they live in Washington, DC. In reality, they live right next
door.

The most obvious bureaucrats work for administrative
agencies, and there are a lot of them. On average, each state
has 150 separately administered agencies.[42] Multiply that
number exponentially to compute the number of local boards
and commissions. But the even bigger—and more rapidly
growing—story is special districts, referred to by one commentator as "the 'new dark continent of American politics.'"[43]
And indeed they are often mysterious and unknowable.

By definition, special districts are autonomous governmental entities formed to provide specific services. The best-known examples are school districts, but there are also special districts that provide roads, tunnels, electricity, transportation, water, sewers, and other public services. Although they exercise the powers of municipal governments, such as taxation, the issuance of revenue bonds, and eminent domain, they are not accountable to other governments and are often unelected. Even when they are elected, voter turnout is notoriously low—often between 2 and 5 percent[44]—because most voters don't know (or care) what these entities are. In 1969, the Greenwood (Texas) Utility District was authorized to issue millions of dollars in bonds in a special election with a total turnout of four voters.[45]

Apart from school districts, there were very few special districts until the New Deal, when President Franklin Delano Roosevelt encouraged their growth as a means of avoiding municipal bankruptcies.[46] Today they are a wildly popular means of exercising governmental power without the ordinary constraints of government. Their growth is nothing short of phenomenal: In 1942, there were only 8,299 special districts apart from school districts[47] in the United States; today there are more than 34,000 (see figure 5). They are multiplying rapidly: The number of special districts increased by 9 percent between 1992 and 1997 alone. They outnumber municipal corporations by two to one and counties by about ten to one.[48] They are often massive: As far back as 1952, the Chicago Transit Authority had more employees than did 17 U.S. states and took in greater revenue than a dozen states.[49] And special districts operate almost completely beneath the radar. As one text on urban politics explains:

> The news media give very little coverage to the meetings and actions of district boards. Very few urban citizens are probably even only marginally aware of the existence of these . . . governmental bodies. When annual property tax

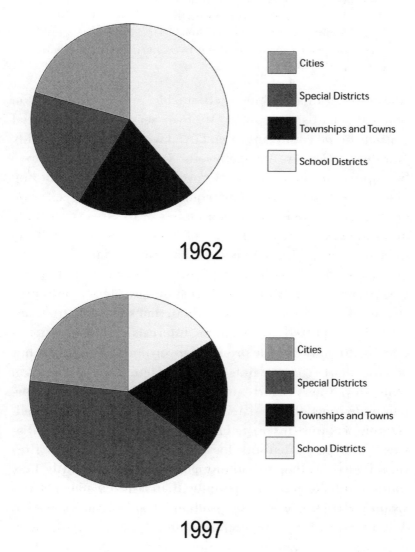

1962

1997

Figure 5   Local Government by Type
Source: U.S. Census Bureau, *Statistical Abstract of the United States* (2000), p. 299.

statements are mailed, few citizens realize just what portion
of their tax bill has been levied by the officials of these low-
visibility special district governments. Popular control over
these district boards is muted further still, as most district
board members are appointed to office and serve staggered
terms in order to insulate them from partisan demands by
elected officials.[50]

As a result, they are often unfathomable, even to experts. One
political scientist recounts, "My own search for the special
districts in the county in which I lived when I began this study
(Middlesex County, Massachusetts) was a complete failure."
She spoke to numerous local government offices, including
planning officials at the state, county, and local levels, "none
of whom could tell me the boundaries of the special districts
in Middlesex County and none of whom could even tell me
the names of the special districts that governed me."[51]

Special districts often are promoted by liberals and "good
government" types who do not trust the private sector to provide public services. It is ironic, then, that special districts are
routinely captured by business interests, for the districts
operate not only outside ordinary government constraints but
outside market constraints as well. Hence in Washington
State, developers eagerly supported the creation of transportation districts in the late 1980s. As one observer noted,
"Developers were interested in these districts because the districts could generate funds for development *and* because they
would give developers almost complete control over how
these funds would be spent."[52] Similarly, water districts
around Houston were the product of an alliance between
developers and the city, both of which desired an entity with
unlimited taxing and borrowing authority.[53] Large bond bro-
kerages also exert enormous influence over special districts
and profit tidily from them.[54]

The lack of governmental and market constraints lends itself not only to patronage and corruption but to some spectacular disasters. In the early 1980s, the Washington Public Power Supply System (whose initials and practices earned it the Wall Street moniker "Whoops") generated $28 billion in outstanding debts, having issued the most widely held tax-exempt bonds in the market. A complete lack of administrative controls led to the largest default in the history of the American municipal bond market up to that point. As political scientist Diana B. Henriques recounts,

> few if any private corporations could grow as fast and as big as WPPSS did without some proof of success and some demonstration of sound management skills. But as WPPSS grew—borrowing its way to behemoth status—it never demonstrated any talent for successfully managing the task it had set for itself.[55]

The problems flowing from the lack of accountability inherent in hidden public authorities, Henriques says, are compounded by the influence of special interests, "because public authorities do the work that is most attractive to those outsiders who are intent on corrupting governments."[56]

Public authorities also provide a convenient means for clever politicians to evade constitutional constraints on government power. As Michael S. Gruen reported in *City Journal*, public authorities often "act as middleman, conducting transactions that would be illegal if the city or state carried them out. These make a mockery of the legal protections that New York voters have enacted to ensure that the business of government is conducted democratically."[57]

For instance, the City of New York can't sell its real property without a public auction. So when it wanted to give city-owned real estate to a nonprofit organization headed by

Andrew Cuomo, former U.S. secretary of housing and urban development and son of the former governor, it couldn't do so without an auction that might have put the property in someone else's hands. So instead the city invited the Urban Development Corporation, a public authority, to condemn the city's property for one dollar—and then to sell it to Cuomo's nonprofit for one dollar. The city charter was evaded, mission accomplished.

Likewise, the New York state constitution provides that no long-term debt can be contracted "by or on behalf of the state" without voter approval by referendum. But the state's record of gaining voter approval was dismal: Between 1975 and 1995, voters approved only $6.5 billion in state debt while rejecting $4.2 billion. So the state used back-door financing to procure an additional $20 billion, using public authorities such as the Urban Development Corporation and the Thruway Authority to do the borrowing instead. Though the scheme is obviously a charade—the state creates new political entities and invests them with powers the state itself does not possess—New York state courts have failed to put an end to it. Concludes Gruen, "Over and over, New York's public officials have seemed to view the State Constitution not as a limit on their power but as a challenge to their talents for evasion."[58]

Although the growth of local governments seems inexorable, there are some countervailing trends that are leaving individuals with more money in their wallets and greater rights. The first is privatization of services, from contracting out schools to transportation, trash hauling, and other services.[59] For example, while serving as mayor of Indianapolis, Steve Goldsmith managed to rein in the city's bloat by designating services for competitive bidding. Even government agencies were allowed to compete; and competition forced them to become more efficient when they won contracts.

Another private alternative is homeowner associations, which deliver certain services to their own residents. Although some homeowners chafe under the oppressive leadership of some HOAs, the entities are based on voluntary contracts, and the costs are borne and controlled by the beneficiaries. Ultimately, their smaller size and commonality of interest make them more efficient and responsive to residents' needs compared to local governments.

Finally, a growing number of people are eschewing city governments altogether, flocking to unincorporated areas that combine county government with private services to reap lower overall taxes and fewer layers of government. Few people know, for example, that 96 percent of the Las Vegas Strip is not within the city of Las Vegas. Rather, it is part of "Paradise," an unincorporated part of Clark County with 186,000 residents.[60] Likewise, hundreds of thousands of people live in unincorporated areas of Fairfax County, Virginia, and Montgomery County, Maryland, in the suburbs of Washington, DC. Many residents who have Alexandria mailing addresses in fact reside in unincorporated parts of Fairfax County.

But local governments are not about to cede their power without a tenacious fight—and they often use tax dollars to wage it. States, cities, mayors, governors, state attorneys general, public universities, and other municipal entities and officials have formed powerful special-interest groups to lobby in Washington, DC, and in state capitols to preserve and expand their hegemony. The National League of Cities, for instance, collects tax-funded dues from 1,800 cities and towns.[61] Its efforts are abetted by public-employee unions such as AFSCME, which resist every effort to reduce the size and scope of state and local governments. AFSCME warns, for instance, that "privatization threatens job security, pay and benefits, working conditions and career opportunities," meaning that "we must all fight privatization . . . before the first warning sign and with every resource."[62]

The sobering reality is that state and local governments have grown in scope and power almost beyond recognition, requiring us to dust away the cobwebs of nostalgia. The trend is rarely remarked upon, yet it affects each and every one of us in intimate and tangible ways. The propensity of local governments toward grassroots tyranny has been recognized since the earliest days of our republic, but never have the implications for individual liberty been more profound than they are today. Fighting city hall has become a David versus Goliath struggle. The real-world consequences stemming from the growth of the local leviathan are the subject of the chapters that follow.

2

Federalism: The Grand Design

It is at all times necessary . . . that we frequently refresh
our patriotism by reference to first principles. It is by trac-
ing things to their origins that we learn to understand
them; and it is by keeping that line and origin always in
view that we never forget them.
—Thomas Paine, *Dissertation on First
Principles of Government* (1775)

THINGS WERE NOT supposed to turn out as they have, with
mushrooming government and concomitant abuses of individual liberty at every level. Our constitutional system was
established to prevent accretions of power, and excesses in
the exercise of power, at every level of government. The system was intended to restrain growth at the federal level, and—
though some find the fact surprising—to restrain abuses of
state and local power. That it has failed in the former is painfully clear; the extent to which it has failed in the latter grows
clearer (and more painful) with each day. To determine how
best to vindicate the framers' goal of a government that in its
totality and all its permutations respects individual liberties

requires a careful analysis of what was intended in the first place, and what mechanisms were erected to constrain the growth and power of government.

Years ago during the Reagan administration, when I was working in the U.S. Department of Justice, I encountered a female colleague while riding the Metro to work. She noticed I was wearing a tie with an Adam Smith insignia—a tell-tale sartorial sign of the ideological true believers within the administration.

My colleague asked if I was a conservative. Not wanting to get into the fine distinctions between libertarians and conservatives, I said yes.

To which she replied, "I dated a conservative once." Wrinkling her nose disdainfully, she added, "All he wanted to do was talk about federalism."

So it is with some trepidation, and at the risk of ruining dating prospects for future generations of conservatives, that I embark upon a discussion of federalism. For better or worse, it is central to the context within which the local leviathan has emerged. And it is equally critical to resolving the conundrum presented by big government at the local level. It is an issue over which liberals and conservatives tenaciously disagree— and yet an issue on which both liberals and conservatives, for the most part, are wrong. All of which makes it, once one delves beneath the surface, a surprisingly interesting topic.[1]

Federalism, wrote Felix Morley in 1959, is "the distinctively American contribution to political art."[2] But what exactly is federalism? The term evokes so much confusion that one scholar of federalism has identified 267 different but overlapping definitions of the term.[3] But despite the confusion and controversy, any serious inquiry into the history and principles of American federalism will reveal, as Daniel J. Elazar has observed, that "the central interest of true federalism in all its species is liberty."[4] Any discussion of federalism that is bereft of concern for liberty divorces the vehicle from its destination.

Federalism was part of the constitutional tapestry designed by our Constitution's framers to create an effective national government while protecting liberty. First, they invested the national government with limited and specifically prescribed powers—only those powers essential for effective governance. They also established specific constraints on government power and recognized specific rights in the Bill of Rights.

They also, as Robert Bork has described it, pursued a "deliberate strategy to create competing centers of power in order to avoid tyranny."[5] Some key elements of this strategy were the separation of powers and the system of checks and balances among the three branches of national government, designed so that each branch could curb the excesses of the others. But perhaps the most significant was the adoption of federalism as the organizational structure of American government. To say the least, it has not always turned out as intended. But, when properly understood and implemented, federalism retains vast potential to operate as a mighty bulwark for liberty.

Federalism at the Founding

When the framers set about the job of creating a federal constitution, they faced a daunting task. Under the Articles of Incorporation, the government seemed incapable of managing the country's affairs. The loose confederation structure had encouraged 13 highly independent states to think of themselves as sovereign entities and not as part of a unified nation. The challenge was to transform this cacophony into harmony without sacrificing the principles over which the American Revolution had been fought.

That entailed three seemingly irreconcilable tasks: to create a national government with sufficient powers to govern effectively, to convince the states to surrender the portion of their autonomy necessary to accomplish that goal, and to achieve all that while vigorously protecting individual liberty.[6]

Fresh from the experience of monarchial oppression, the framers were united in their distrust of a strong central government, and they viewed the states as essential to the preservation of freedom. Edward S. Corwin observes that colonial experience had demonstrated that "the best protection of the rights of the individual was to be found in the hard-won prerogatives of the colonial legislatures against the royal governors."[7] Indeed, most state constitutions contained express protections of individual liberty.

This view of states as guardians of individual liberty provided one of the baseline premises of American federalism. As James Madison declared, even "the greatest opponents to a Federal Government admit the State Legislatures to be sure guardians of the people's liberty."[8] But the framers also recognized that the states themselves were capable of tyranny. After all, they were governments too. "The smaller the society," remarked Madison, the perceptive political scientist, "the smaller the number of individuals composing a majority, and . . . the more easily they will concert and execute their plans of oppression."[9] Indeed, one of the principal motivations for drawing up the Constitution was the common practice—allowed under the Articles of Confederation—of state governments to erect protectionist trade barriers, thwarting free trade among the states.[10] "The great and radical vice in the construction of the existing Confederation," charged Alexander Hamilton, "is in the principle of legislation for states and governments, in their corporate or collective capacities, as contradistinguished from the individuals of which they consist."[11]

Hence in the new constitution, not only would states act as guarantors of liberty, but the national government would operate as a check against tyrannical impulses by state governments. As Professor John Yoo explains, "By allowing, or even encouraging, the federal and state governments to check each other, the Framers' Constitution seeks to create an area of liberty that cannot be regulated by either government."[12] For the framers, the goal of federalism was not to glorify one level of government over another, but to effectuate the surest possible safeguards for freedom. The core value was liberty; the seminal threat to that value was government in all its forms.

Some commentators, such as Robert Bork, perceive federalism as a mechanism to effectuate majority will. To the contrary, the framers understood that the greatest threat to liberty was the people themselves. As Madison warned in a letter to Thomas Jefferson,

> Wherever the real power in a Government lies, there is the danger of oppression. In our Governments the real power lies in the majority of the Community, and the invasion of private rights is chiefly to be apprehended, not from acts of Government contrary to the sense of its constituents, but from acts in which the Government is the mere instrument of the major number of the constituents.[13]

Consequently, checks and balances among governments were insufficient to protect liberty; substantive protections were necessary as well. "The prescriptions in favor of liberty ought to be levelled against that quarter where the greatest danger lies," urged Madison. "But this is not found in either the Executive or Legislative departments of government, but in the body of the people, operating by the majority against the minority."[14]

Such instances of majoritarian tyranny would be advanced through the emergence of the "faction," which Madison defined in his magnificent *Federalist* No. 10 as "a number of citizens . . . who are united and actuated by some common impulse of passion, or of interest, adverse to the rights of other citizens, or to the permanent and aggregate interests of the community."[15] To preserve liberty, Madison warned, factions "must be rendered . . . unable to concert and carry into effect schemes of oppression."[16]

Thus, for Madison, "To secure the public good and private rights against the danger of such a faction, and at the same time to preserve the spirit of popular government" were the "great object" of republican government.[17] To that end, observed Felix Morley, the founders "devised a balanced political structure, designed to protect minorities against the majority, right down to that minority of one, the individual."[18] Though it's often pressed into service by apologists of oppression, as Yale law professor Akhil Reed Amar explains, "the Constitution's political structure of federalism and sovereignty is designed to protect, not defeat, its legal substance of individual rights."[19] Federalism, which balances the power of the national government against that of the states and limits the powers of both, is an integral part of the overall constitutional structure calculated to maximize individual liberty within the framework of effective government.

Federalism in the Original Design

One conundrum the framers faced in constructing the new national constitution was the question of sovereignty. Under the Articles of Confederation, the states were sovereign; and this presented the biggest obstacle to effective national union. To make the national government sovereign would require states to sacrifice powers they were reluctant to surrender. But to maintain state sovereignty would deprive the national government of the power it needed to achieve the framers' objectives.

The framers solved the dilemma through a truly revolutionary innovation: Sovereignty, they determined, resided in neither the national nor state governments, but in the people. The founder credited with the solution, Robert Wilson, declared that the concept of popular sovereignty was so central that without it "we shall never be able to understand the principle on which this system was constructed."[20] Madison likewise argued that debate over national versus state sovereignty missed the point entirely. "These gentlemen must here be reminded of their error," Madison remarked. "They must be told that the ultimate authority . . . resides in the people alone."[21]

Grounded in the concept of popular sovereignty, the Constitution took the form of a social contract, whereby the people surrendered only so much of their autonomy as was necessary to create a government of carefully delimited powers. In that system, Madison explained, the "Federal and State governments are in fact but different agents and trustees of the people," and both are subject to a "common superior"— the people.[22]

Hence, the people delegated to the national government specific powers, such as the powers to regulate commerce among the states and to declare war. Moreover, the framers erected obstacles to the accretion of national government power, such as the separation of powers among the three branches of government, and the election of U.S. senators by state legislatures. This division of powers was intended to protect individual liberty. As Justice Anthony Kennedy has observed, "The Framers split the atom of sovereignty. It was the genius of their idea that our citizens would have two political capacities, one state and one federal, each protected from incursion by the other."[23]

Madison viewed two institutions as essential in protecting individual rights against national power: the federal courts and the state legislatures. The federal courts, Madison declared, would serve as "the guardians of those rights; they will be an impenetrable bulwark against every assumption of power in the legislature or executive; [and] they will be naturally led to resist every encroachment upon rights expressly stipulated for in the constitution by the declaration of rights."[24] Likewise, Madison predicted that "the State Legislatures will jealously and closely watch the operations of [national] government, and be able to resist with more effect every assumption of power."[25]

But, as Madison argued at the Constitutional Convention, the national government also has to possess sufficient powers to protect "the rights of the minority," which are placed at risk "in all cases where a majority are united by a common interest or passion."[26] Hence the Constitution invested the national government with certain powers to protect against violations of individual liberty by state governments. Foremost among them was the power given to Congress to regulate interstate commerce. As Robert Bork has observed, "one of the major reasons for holding the Philadelphia Convention was the states' interference with national trade."[27] States had erected parochial trade barriers to protect local industries, and it was painfully clear that the states could not police themselves. As a result, the commerce clause was created to ensure free trade among the states.

Moreover, the Constitution established several express

limitations on state power. Article IV, for instance, established that the "Citizens of each State shall be entitled to all Privileges and Immunities of Citizens in the several States." Article I, section 10, created additional limitations. As Madison described them, "Bills of attainder, *ex-post-facto* laws, and laws impairing the obligation of contracts, are contrary to the first principles of the social compact." Their express prohibition in the Constitution, he remarked, provides a "constitutional bulwark in favor of personal security and private rights."[28]

The dual allocation of powers to the national and state governments provided the principal protection for individual liberty in the original constitution. As Alexander Hamilton argued, "This balance between the national and State governments . . . is of utmost importance. It forms a double security for the people."[29] That theme was further explained in *The Federalist*:

> In a single republic, all power surrendered by the people is submitted to the administration of a single government; and usurpations are guarded against by a division of the government into distinct and separate departments. In the compound government of America, the power surrendered by the people is first divided between two distinct governments, and then the portion allotted to each subdivided among the distinct and separate departments. Hence a double security arises to the rights of the people. The different governments will control each other, at the same time that each will be controlled by itself.[30]

As Madison summarized it, within this compound government with its balance and division of powers, each level of government would have the ability "to resist and frustrate the measures of each other."[31] Not exactly a recipe for efficient government, but a necessity given the framers' overarching concern about oppressive government.

From this basic original constitutional structure and from the framers' original intent, it is clear that no effort was made to elevate one level of government over another. To the national government were delegated specifically enumerated and limited powers, with the states retaining the remainder of the legitimate powers of government. But the central value animating the design was individual liberty, which necessitated express limits on the power of national and state governments alike. Those protections for liberty were strengthened with subsequent modifications to the original constitution, first in the Bill of Rights and a century later with the ratification of the 14th Amendment.

The Bill of Rights

The framers' original design was amplified in the first ten amendments to the original constitution, upon which ratification of the document was conditioned. The central argument of the libertarian "anti-federalists" was that the proposed constitution contained inadequate safeguards for individual rights. George Mason warned that the "laws of the general government being paramount to the laws and constitutions of the several States, the declarations of rights in the separate States are no security."[32]

The gist of the anti-federalist objection was the absence of a bill of rights, to protect individuals not as citizens of their respective states but as Americans. Madison initially opposed a bill of rights, fearing that to enumerate specific rights would be to undermine the existence and protection of rights not expressly enumerated. But eventually he acquiesced and a bill of rights was appended to the original constitution.

The first eight amendments set forth specific rights and explicitly restrained the power of the national government to violate them. The more general Ninth and Tenth Amendments, by contrast, created a hierarchy of rights and government power. The Ninth Amendment was intended to answer Madison's concern by making it clear that the first eight amendments were not a complete catalogue of individual liberties. It reads, "The enumeration in the Constitution, of certain rights, shall not be construed to deny or disparage others retained by the People." As Randy Barnett explains, "only a handful of the many rights proposed by state ratification conventions were eventually incorporated into the Bill of Rights. The Ninth Amendment was offered precisely to 'compensate' . . . critics for the absence of an extended list of rights."[33]

The framers' understanding of individual rights was informed largely by British common law. As Barnett argues, "The freedom to act within the boundaries provided by one's common law rights may be viewed as a central background presumption of the Constitution—a presumption that is reflected in the Ninth Amendment."[34]

In the same fashion, the scope of permissible government authority was circumscribed for the framers by the common law concept of the "police power"—expressed in the preamble to the Constitution as the power to "establish Justice, insure domestic Tranquility, provide for the common defence, promote the general Welfare, and secure the Blessings of Liberty to ourselves and our Posterity." The relative apportionment of powers between the national and state governments was expressed in the Tenth Amendment, which provides, "The powers not delegated to the United States by the Constitution, nor prohibited by it to the States, are reserved to the States respectively, or to the people." In other words, the national government was delegated only those express powers enumerated in the Constitution, while all other legitimate powers of government were retained by the states. But the Tenth Amendment also made clear that the ultimate source of government power was the people themselves. As constitutional scholar Ronald D. Rotunda has put it, "The Framers created federalism not so much to protect the states but to protect the people."[35]

Both the Ninth and Tenth Amendments, Barnett argues, "can be viewed as establishing a general constitutional presumption of individual liberty."[36] By its plain meaning, the Ninth Amendment suggests that if the Constitution does not expressly grant a power to the national government, the government does not possess that power. At the same time, the Tenth Amendment implies a preference for decentralized governmental powers, residing either in the states or the people themselves. Sadly, both presumptions are largely reversed today, as we shall see.

Still, the provisions of the original constitution, buttressed by the Bill of Rights, created the initial machinery of federalism that was intended not to create a protective shield for abuses of individual rights by state governments, but as a means to protect individual rights against all domestic governments. This concept of federalism established a hierarchy of values, with liberty first and foremost. Within that constitutional system, states were seen as a means to an end rather than an end in themselves: States were viewed as the natural guardians of the individual rights of the citizens, with the national government stepping in only in limited instances (such as interstate commerce and the sanctity of contracts) where the states could not be relied upon to restrain themselves.

The presumption that states would protect rather than violate individual rights proved, of course, horribly erroneous. So, less than a century after its ratification, the Constitution was brought in for a repair job that would correct a gaping flaw in the original document, complete the machinery of federalism, and provide greater and more enduring safeguards for the protection of individual liberty against governmental despotism.

Perfecting the Design: The 14th Amendment

Four basic premises regarding individual liberty supported the original construct of federalism: that the national and state governments would each effectively balance and restrain the power of the other; that the federal courts would strike down invasions of individual liberty; that state legislatures and constitutions would provide an effective bulwark for individual freedom; and that the Bill of Rights would provide security for individual liberty. To the contrary, clashes between national and state power were a constant feature of the period leading up to the Civil War, and the national and state governments were not up to the task of restraining one another's excesses. Federal courts abetted rather than prevented abuses of individual rights. State constitutions proved to be of little force against deprivations of rights. And the Bill of Rights provided no constraint against abuses by state and local governments.

The starkest example of the deprivation of liberty, of course, was the institution of human slavery, whose legality was implicitly sanctioned by the original constitution even as it violated every principle upon which that document was based. But the seeds of national abdication of the protection of individual rights were sown in a different context. In *Barron v. Mayor and City Council of Baltimore* in 1833, a resident challenged in federal court the city's actions that resulted in

the destruction of the value of a wharf, claiming a violation of
the Fifth Amendment. The Bill of Rights, ruled Chief Justice
John Marshall, provided "security against the apprehended
encroachments of the general government—not against those
of local governments."[37] The federal courts would provide no
recourse against violations of basic civil rights by state or local
governments, thereby repudiating the notion implicit in the
Constitution that individuals were vested with a broad range
of natural rights and that all governments were circumscribed
in their power to invade those rights.

By reinforcing the concept of state sovereignty with regard
to the recognition and protection of individual rights, the *Barron*
decision fueled arguments made by pro-slavery activists
that attempts to restrain slavery trenched against "states'
rights." The leading pro-slavery advocate, John C. Calhoun,
"denied generally the doctrine of natural rights in the traditional context, and converted the principle of states' rights
into an instrumentality . . . , with the protection of slavery
foremost in his consideration," recounts historian Robert J.
Harris. "In so doing he extracted from states' rights principles
most of the vestiges of revolutionary and natural rights philos-
ophy."[38] In this formulation, states were transformed from
guardians of individual liberty into guardians of human slavery, and state power as an end in itself became a mantra. The
federal constitution and the courts trusted with its enforcement were helpless to intercede. And any action that inter-
fered with states' rights could be "nullified," because in the
federal system, states (rather than individuals) were sovereign.
Through this logic, the entire construct of federalism was
twisted beyond recognition, and the battle lines were drawn.

By implicitly embracing Calhoun's revisionist principles
in *Barron*, the Supreme Court laid the groundwork for its subsequent infamous *Dred Scott* decision, in which an emanci-

pated black man sought to invoke federal jurisdiction for the protection of his civil rights. The Court rejected the claim, ruling that blacks had "no rights or privileges but such as those who held the power and the government might choose to grant them."[39] The federal judicial abdication was complete.

Meanwhile, Southern states aggressively enacted laws restricting freedom of speech and press in an effort to suppress antislavery agitation. States also passed laws requiring local postmasters to intercept abolitionist propaganda, and local governments refused to provide police protection to abolitionists against mob violence.[40] Plainly, states were becoming agents of wide-ranging oppression, rather than serving their constitutional role of protecting individual liberty.

But those who used state and local government for oppression were sowing the seeds of their own demise. Statesmen who remained true to natural-rights principles began questioning the premise that states were adequate guardians of individual rights. As commentator Harold M. Hyman observes, "The antislavery champions perceived correctly that injustices were overwhelmingly local and state, that federal justice had been irrelevant as a remedy, and that dual federalism had failed" in its mission of protecting liberty.[41] The struggle over slavery convinced Northerners that "it was the states, and not the federal government, that presented the greatest threat to individual liberties."[42]

By withdrawing from the Union, the South repudiated a constitutional system dedicated to individual liberty and embraced an ideology that glorified state over individual rights. In the aftermath of the Civil War, the victors were determined to correct the constitutional inadequacies that had allowed states to run roughshod over individual liberties.

Ultimately, as J. M. Balkin recounts, this "new way of think-ing" about states as violators rather than guardians of individ-ual liberty manifested itself in the 14th Amendment, which "drastically altered the balance of power between the states and the federal government."[43]

The Reconstruction Congress was unlike any other, before or since. Because the Southern states were excluded for a time, Congress was overwhelmingly dominated by a sin-gle party, a clear and coherent vision of natural rights, and a goal of constitutional revision in accord with those principles. As legal historian Michael Kent Curtis remarks, "perhaps the most common Republican refrain in the Congress was that life, liberty, and property of American citizens must be pro-tected against denial by the states."[44]

The concern was not a hypothetical one. As soon as the war ended, Southern legislatures reacted to the end of slavery by enacting "black codes," designed to prevent newly eman-cipated blacks from enforcing contracts, owning property, and pursuing trades and professions. Congress responded with the Civil Rights Act of 1866, whose goal, in the words of Sen. Lyman Trumbull, was to ensure for all persons "the right to the fruit of their own labor, the right to make contracts, the right to buy and sell, and enjoy liberty and happiness."[45] Pres-ident Andrew Johnson questioned congressional authority to limit the power of the states, which led Congress to "consti-tutionalize" the provisions of the Civil Rights Act of 1866 in the 14th Amendment. Ratified in 1868, the amendment pro-vides in relevant part:

> no State shall make or enforce any law which shall abridge the privileges or immunities of citizens of the United States; nor shall any State deprive any person of life, liberty, or property, without due process of law; nor deny to any per-son the equal protection of the laws.

Congress followed up with the Civil Rights Act of 1871, which provided a private cause of action for those who had been deprived of their federally protected rights "under color of [state law]."

Congress recognized that it was embarking upon a radical remaking of national and state powers, designed to create a more effective safeguard for individual rights. As Rep. William Lawrence expressed it, the new national protections of individual rights were "scarcely less to the people of this country than the Magna Charta was to the people of England."[46] Whereas the original constitution assigned to states the primary role of protecting fundamental individual rights, a co-equal role now was assigned to the national government. Under the Tenth Amendment, states were still empowered to provide greater protections of individual rights than the national government might provide; but under the 14th Amendment, the national government obtained for the first time the clear power to curb state abuses of rights. And within that scheme, the federal courts were assigned critical new powers.

The Fourteenth Amendment was intended to put the finishing touches on the constitutional framework for federalism. The provisions of the Ninth, Tenth, and Fourteenth Amendments demonstrate a clear preference for leaving decision-making with local government—as long as that doesn't result in threats to individual autonomy. Each level of government is empowered to check the other whenever that other exceeds the boundaries of its power and infringes on individual rights.

The object of federalism, properly understood, is liberty. The framers both of the original constitution and of the 14th Amendment had a firm grasp on that understanding. In the 20th century, a great deal of confusion about federalism emerged, among both the ideological right and the ideological left, as the next chapter will illustrate. That confusion created an environment in which grassroots tyranny has flourished. For this reason, it is imperative that, in the 21st century, we rediscover and reclaim the original principles of federalism, and invoke it as a powerful doctrine on behalf of individual liberty, rather than as a justification for local tyranny.

3

The Curious
Evolution of
Federalism

IN THE LATTER third of the 20th century, federalism would
become a centerpiece of American jurisprudence—yet at the
hands of both liberals and conservatives, it evolved into often
unrecognizable forms, and failed to consistently achieve its
goal of promoting individual liberty. In the hands of some liberals, federalism provided a convenient rhetorical rationale
for expanded state power. In the hands of some conservatives,
states' rights once again became an end in itself, regardless of
whether it advanced liberty. This philosophical confusion has
had the pernicious and predictable effect of reducing important structural limitations on the scope of state and local government power, and on abuses of that power.

The path to the present has been circuitous. The undoing of federalism began swiftly after the enactment of the 14th Amendment. The U.S. Supreme Court quickly received an opportunity to give meaning to the amendment by using it to restrict tyranny by state governments. But in one of the worst decisions in the history of American jurisprudence, the Court blew it badly.

All three provisions of the 14th Amendment were important. The due process clause expressly limited the states' power to infringe upon life, liberty, and property. The equal protection clause provided a safeguard against the evils of "faction" that Madison had warned about. But it was the amendment's first provision—the privileges or immunities clause—that was intended to protect substantive rights against infringement by state governments, particularly the liberties that had been protected by the Civil Rights Act of 1866.[1]

But before the ink on the 14th Amendment was barely dry, the Supreme Court, in a 5-4 decision in 1873, gutted the privileges or immunities clause in the *Slaughter-House Cases*. The cases involved a bribery-procured Louisiana slaughterhouse monopoly challenged by a group of butchers it had put out of business. The majority ruled that the clause was designed to protect only the rights of former slaves and those rights created by virtue of federal citizenship, such as the rights of habeas corpus and of access to navigable waters. In dissent, Justice Stephen Field declared that if such a paltry list of rights was all that the privileges or immunities clause was meant to protect, the 14th Amendment "was a vain and idle enactment, which accomplished nothing, and most unnecessarily excited Congress upon its passage."[2] Field lamented the decision, "for by it the right of free labor, one of the most sacred and imprescriptible rights of man, is vio-lated."[3]

By removing constitutional protection for freedom of con-tract, *Slaughter-House* paved the way for the shameful subse-quent 1896 decision in *Plessy v. Ferguson*,[4] in which the Supreme Court upheld a state law requiring "separate but equal" streetcar seating.[5] *Plessy* was a test case funded by the streetcar company to challenge the inefficient and discrimi-natory restrictions. Because freedom of contract—one of the essential "privileges or immunities" of citizenship—had been eviscerated by *Slaughter-House*, the plaintiffs were forced to rely on a more difficult equal-protection challenge. The Court rejected the challenge by an 8-1 vote, opening the door to Jim Crow laws and decades of subjugation of blacks by govern-ments at every level. Though *Plessy* would be overturned 58 years later in *Brown v. Board of Education*,[6] the *Slaughter-House Cases* remain on the books today, nullifying the great promise of the 14th Amendment as a substantive guarantor of funda-mental individual rights against abuses by state governments.

Still, over the years, the Court has breathed some life into the 14th Amendment, though all too selectively. Creating a concept called "substantive due process"—a concept made necessary due to the evisceration of the privileges or immu-nities clause in *Slaughter-House*—a conservative Court prior to the New Deal used the due process clause to shield busi-ness activities from arbitrary or excessive economic regulation by the states,[7] and to protect such personal liberties as the right of parents to direct and control the education of their children.[8] When liberals gained control of the Court in the 1930s, they jettisoned judicial protection for economic lib-erty,[9] and instead used the due process clause to "incorpo-rate" some (but not all) of the protections of the Bill of Rights into the 14th Amendment. Specifically, the Court applied to the states protections it deemed "fundamental to the American scheme of justice," such as freedom of speech and press, free exercise of religion, freedom against self-incrimination, and freedom against unreasonable searches and seizures.[10] In more recent years, a more conservative Court has scaled back those protections somewhat, but has applied the "takings clause" of the Fifth Amendment to increase scrutiny of excessive regulation of private property by state and local governments.[11] This uneven record demonstrates that neither liberal nor conservative justices have a consistent approach to judicial protection of individual liberties or a coherent grasp on the purposes of federalism.

Liberal Judicial Activism

Liberal judicial activism is legion and legendary. The use of judicial power for the ends of "social justice"[12] has taken many forms: the creation of welfare entitlements and sweeping criminal rights; the invention of two tiers of rights, fundamental and nonfundamental; the recognition of concepts unknown to the Constitution such as "separation of church and state"; the assumption of legislative and executive powers such as judicial taxation and the operation of school and prison systems; and the derivation of rights not from constitutional text or intent but from "emanations flowing from penumbras." The left's unbounded judicial adventurism and its failure to exercise any judicial self-restraint inflicted incalculable harm to the integrity and reputation of courts, and led to a predictable backlash that helped elect Richard Nixon and Ronald Reagan and ultimately produced the Rehnquist Court.[13]

But perhaps the most remarkable example of the left's ends-justifies-the-means jurisprudence was its turnabout on federalism. Throughout the Franklin D. Roosevelt administration and the subsequent Warren era of the Supreme Court, liberals displayed utter contempt for federalism, invoking Congress's power to regulate commerce as a justification for sweeping national power. Indeed, as early as 1940, the liberal Court dismissed the Tenth Amendment as a mere "truism."[14]

But despite disavowing original intent with respect to federalism, liberals perceived value in some degree of state autonomy even early on. As Robert H. Freilich describes it, "Federalism preserves the states not for the purpose of diluting the power of the national government in domestic issues or of overriding minority interests in our society, but of encouraging creativity in government."[15] In other words, federalism was not, as the framers intended, a means by which to limit the power of government, but rather to ensure that state power in the service of "creative" ends would be just as open-ended as the power of the national government.

This liberal version of federalism traces its origins to early 20th-century jurisprudence, when conservatives dominated the Supreme Court and occasionally struck down economic regulations as violations of individual liberty. In its 1932 decision in *New State Ice Co. v. Liebmann*, for instance, the Court struck down an Oklahoma law that prohibited the manufacture or sale of ice without a showing of public convenience and necessity and approval by a state regulatory board. Dissenting, Justice Louis Brandeis articulated the liberal view of federalism:

> There must be power in the States . . . to remould, through experimentation, our economic practices to meet changing social and economic needs. . . . It is one of the happy incidents of the federal system that a single courageous State may, if its citizens choose, serve as a laboratory.[16]

Brandeis didn't explain how it is "courageous" for a state to indulge protectionist sentiments and destroy a person's livelihood. His views were rejected by the Court's majority, speaking through Justice George Sutherland, who declared, "The principle is embedded in our constitutional system that there are certain essentials of liberty with which the state is not entitled to dispense in the interest of experiments."[17] Unfortunately, Brandeis's views would quickly gain ascendancy, and would retain it to this day.

The leading modern theorist of liberal federalism was Justice William Brennan, one of the leading architects of the Warren Court jurisprudence from the 1950s to the 1970s, who remained during the shift to a more conservative Court. Initially, Brennan had little use for federalism, rejecting assertions of "states' rights" and glorifying national power. In a law review article written in 1964, during the heyday of the Warren era, Brennan urged state courts to broadly interpret federal law, because "the fundamental obligation to administer federal law rests on both [federal and state] courts," which possess an "identity of underlying purpose."[18] But by 1977, when the Supreme Court began to change course, Brennan suddenly discovered the virtue of federalism.[19] Calling himself a "devout believer" in federalism,[20] Brennan urged that

> state courts cannot rest when they have afforded their own citizens the full protections of the federal Constitution. State constitutions, too, are a font of individual liberties, their protections often extending beyond those required by the Supreme Court's interpretation of federal law. The legal revolution which has brought federal law to the fore must not be allowed to inhibit the independent protective force of state law. . . .[21]

Indeed, Brennan proclaimed, the "rediscovery by state supreme courts of the broader protections afforded their own citizens by their state Constitutions . . . is probably the most important development in constitutional jurisprudence of our times."[22] Viewed as independent sources of judicial power, Brennan would subsequently observe, state constitutions could be used to advance "the aspiration to social justice" and "egalitarianism."[23]

Examples of the Brennan doctrine of federalism abound. The Supreme Court, for instance, rejected the argument that unequal educational funding violates the Constitution, or that there is a federal constitutional right to education at all.[24] But at the behest of liberal advocacy groups, several state courts have recognized under their own constitutions a cause of action for educational equity and equal funding.[25]

Likewise, in 1972, the Supreme Court ruled that under the First Amendment, which applies by its terms to governmental conduct only, individuals do not have a right to engage in petitioning in privately owned shopping centers.[26] Justice Brennan would later complain that the Court had found the First Amendment "insufficiently flexible" to meet the needs of an "evolving society."[27]

But fortunately for advocates of liberal federalism, the California Supreme Court saw things differently, interpreting its own constitution to compel owners of private shopping centers to permit access for petitioning.[28] When the shopping center owners went to the U.S. Supreme Court to protect their own free speech and private-property rights, they were rebuffed in an opinion written not by Brennan, but by the Court's most conservative justice, William H. Rehnquist. Indulging his own deference to states' rights, Rehnquist acknowledged that "there literally has been a 'taking'" of the owners' "right to exclude others," but he concluded that a state may "exercise its police power or its sovereign right to adopt in its own Constitution individual liberties more expan-

sive than those conferred by the Federal Constitution."[29]
Delighted that a conservative advocate of federalism could be
convinced to articulate the liberal vision of federalism, Justice
Thurgood Marshall wrote separately to "applaud the court's
decision, which is part of a very healthy trend of affording
state constitutional provisions a more expansive interpretation than this Court has given to the Federal Constitution."[30]

The liberal view, as articulated by Louis Brandeis, William Brennan, and liberal academics, might properly be
described as "situational federalism," for its proponents
essentially defer to state prerogatives except when they don't.
This convenient divorcing of the concept of federalism from
its underlying purposes—decentralizing governmental decision-making and protecting individual liberty—has contributed to the contemporary quagmire that engulfs federalism. It
has helped transform federalism from a doctrine of liberty
into a tool for expanding government. In the hands of unprin-
cipled liberal activists, federalism suffers an identity crisis,
and its utility as a protective force for freedom is waning.

States' Rights Conservatism

Those who champion federalism as a doctrine of state sovereignty typically refer to themselves as devotees of "original
intent." The preeminent theorist of this movement, Raoul
Berger, places the framers' intent "even above the text" of the
Constitution.[31] But in reality, observes legal scholar Stephen
Macedo, that view of the Constitution "really comes down to
. . . the Jurisprudence of Selective Intent," in which original
intent is vindicated "only when the process serves a deeper
political commitment—that of construing government powers and the powers of majorities broadly and individual rights
narrowly."[32]

This construct of the Constitution as a charter of majoritarianism is curious given constitutional intent and text. The original constitution was undemocratic, with state legislatures choosing U.S. senators rather than direct election, the Electoral College choosing the president, super-majority requirements for various enactments, and all manner of checks and balances designed to frustrate legislation and protect individual liberty.

In their conception of federalism, states' rights conservatives tend to glorify the Tenth Amendment and ignore completely the Ninth Amendment (and for that matter, the remainder of the Bill of Rights as well as the 14th Amendment). Take for example the constitutional analysis of Robert Bork, a leading adherent of the majoritarian school of thought. For Bork, the Tenth Amendment sets forth a clear constitutional command, in that it

> confirms that federal powers were intended to be limited and that the powers not lodged in the national government remained with the states, if the states had such powers under their own constitutions, and, if not, the powers were still held by the people.[33]

In stark contrast, the Ninth Amendment, written in equally broad and general terms, presents to Bork an unfathomable mystery. As Bork testified at his Supreme Court confirmation hearings,

> I do not think you can use the Ninth Amendment unless you know something of what it means. For example, if you had an amendment that says "Congress shall make no" and then there is an inkblot, and you cannot read the rest of it, . . . I do not think the court can make up what might be under the inkblot.[34]

Such a reading of the Ninth Amendment is insupportable.

"Construing the ninth amendment as a mere declaration of constitutional truism, devoid of enforceable content, renders its substance nugatory and assigns to its framers an intention to engage in a purely moot exercise," declares law professor Calvin R. Massey. "This view is at odds with the contextual historical evidence and the specific, articulated concerns of its framers."[35]

States' rights conservatives like Bork trace their conception of federalism not to the Constitution's framers, but to theorists like John C. Calhoun. States' rights conservatives do not view the Constitution as a social contract between individuals and their government, but rather as an act consummated by independent, sovereign states who are little affected by the Constitution's limitations.[36] For Bork, the "protection of individual liberty" is not the central purpose of federalism, but merely an "important benign aspect." But Bork's conception of liberty consists not of any limitation on the power of state governments; rather it lies in the fact that "if another state allows the liberty you value, you can move there."[37] Surely it would have been news to the American founders to learn that the liberties they cherished were not universal or transcendent, but rather subject to the whims of the majority in each particular geographic enclave.

States' rights conservatives reach their goal through a deft rhetorical sleight of hand. Acknowledging the premise of the framers (expressly stated in the Tenth Amendment) that sovereignty lies in the people, they proclaim loudly the people's "right to self-government."[38] From there, however, they go on to define self-government not in the obvious manner—the right of individuals to be masters of their own destinies—but as the power to construct majorities in order to govern others. Contending ahistorically that "the original Constitution was devoted primarily to the mechanisms of democratic choice,"

Bork concludes that "the major freedom . . . of our kind of society is the freedom to choose to have a public morality."[39] As for other "[l]iberties that are deeply rooted in our history and tradition," those are "matters the Founders left to the legislature, either because they assumed no legislature would be mad enough to do away with them or because they wished to allow the legislature discretion to regulate the area as they saw fit."[40]

In such a conceptual framework, constitutional guarantees of freedom of speech, religion, or private-property rights are mere suggestions to legislatures and popular majorities. Unfortunately, as the succeeding chapters will show, legislatures routinely are sufficiently "mad" to violate such precious liberties, with frequency and impunity. Happily, we have a republic, not a democracy; and the courts have not fully accepted the invitation to abdicate their duty within our constitutional framework to protect individual liberties against majoritarian tyranny.

At bottom, states' rights conservatives confuse means and ends. State autonomy under our system of federalism was not conceived as an end in itself, providing carte blanche authority to states to invade individual rights with impunity. Rather, it was intended as a means to securing individual liberty. When federalism is employed to shield state deprivations of individual liberty—whether the institution of human slavery in the 18th century or myriad instances of grassroots tyranny today—it subverts the purposes of federalism. As Professor Amar aptly puts it, "Whenever the rhetoric of 'states' rights' is deployed to defend states' wrongs, our servants have become our masters; our rescuers, our captors."[41] Freedom-loving conservatives need to resuscitate the true intent of federalism and wield it in service of fundamental individual liberties.

The Supreme Court's Federalism

Considering the schizophrenia among conservatives and
liberals regarding federalism, it is little wonder that the
Supreme Court's modern federalism jurisprudence is often
incoherent and inconsistent. Occasionally, the underlying
purposes of federalism peek through the muddled rhetoric,
but typically the battle comes down to a clash between the
respective spheres of national and state power, with sides
chosen up not on the basis of which is consistent with the
underlying libertarian values of federalism, but on whether
the justices prefer state or national power in a particular
instance.

Having dispatched federalism as a "truism," the Court
found little vitality in the Tenth Amendment for many
decades following the New Deal. The debate over federalism
began to resurface in the 1970s as conservatives on the Court
began to gain ascendancy. But instead of breathing new life
into the libertarian principles underlying federalism, the conservatives have tended to attach themselves to notions of
states' rights. Though the Court should "recognize that federalism is for citizens, not states," remarks constitutional
scholar Michael Greve, "[a]ll too often, . . . the Court has
retreated from that insight into a kind of neo-Confederate
romanticism."[42]

Contemporary federalism jurisprudence traces to two
landmark cases, *National League of Cities v. Usery*[43] and *Garcia
v. San Antonio Metropolitan Transit Authority*,[44] in which the
liberal/conservative argument over national power versus
states' rights played out in predictable fashion. In the 1976
National League of Cities case, the Supreme Court confronted
an attempt by Congress to extend the minimum-wage and
maximum-hours provisions of the Fair Labor Standards Act

to employees of state and local governments. (It is revealingly ironic how frequently governments seek to exempt themselves from their own and one another's regulations, but that is a story for another book.) Thus was presented a choice between the power of the national government to regulate employer/employee relationships on the one hand, and the right of state governments and their employees to freely bargain over the terms and conditions of employment on the other.

Justice William Rehnquist, the most consistent states' rights conservative on the Court, writing for a 5-4 majority, struck down on federalism grounds the imposition of federal law, holding that Congress could not directly regulate traditional state functions. Rather than buttressing his decision by noting the federal law's interference with individual liberty, he explicitly repudiated any liberty-based conception of federalism. In fact, he declared that the decision would be altogether different if the regulations were addressed to private rather than state employers. "It is one thing to recognize the authority of Congress to enact laws regulating individual businesses," he stated, but "it is quite another to uphold a similar exercise of congressional authority directed, not to private citizens, but to States as States."[45] The dichotomy illustrates the logical consequence of states' rights federalism: National regulation of private economic activities is permissible, no matter how extensive or injurious; but national regulation of traditional state functions is impermissible, no matter how important its purpose or how insubstantial its effect.

Rehnquist's decision to eschew the libertarian underpinnings of the Tenth Amendment allowed dissenting Justice William Brennan to chastise him for "differentiating 'the people' from 'the States'" under that constitutional provision.[46] Brennan also insisted that limits on the national power to reg-

ulate commerce were found in the political process and not in
the judicial process,[47] sounding more than a bit like a Borkian
apostle of majoritarianism and judicial restraint.

Once conservatives removed federalism from its foundations in concern for individual liberty, they jettisoned the only
principled basis on which to establish any meaningful structural limits on national government power. That would come
back to haunt them only nine years later in *Garcia*, which
marked a serious setback for federalism. In *Garcia*, a metropolitan transit authority sought exemption from the provisions of the Fair Labor Standards Act. This time, a 5-4
majority discarded the *National League of Cities* "traditional
state functions" framework as unworkable and upheld imposition of the federal regulations.

Writing for the majority, Justice Harry Blackmun found
that congressional authority to regulate commerce was essentially boundless, and that "the principal and basic limit" was
not the judicial enforcement of the Tenth Amendment, but
rather "the built-in restraints that our system provides
through state participation in federal action"[48] — in other
words, the good old political process.

The liberals' reasoning in *Garcia* hoisted the states' rights
conservatives on their own majoritarian petard. States' rights
conservatives were aghast that the majority would leave states
no refuge for the protection of their rights other than the
rough and tumble of the political process, even though those
conservatives often would have no such concern with respect
to assertions of individual rights against authoritarian state
laws.

Perhaps recognizing the need to place the case for federalism on more solid and congenial constitutional moorings,
Justice Lewis Powell set forth in his dissent a cogent explica-
tion of the true foundations of federalism. The Court's ruling,

Powell charged, "effectively reduces the Tenth Amendment to meaningless rhetoric,"[49] an outcome he viewed as tragic in that "judicial enforcement of the Tenth Amendment is essential to maintaining the federal system so carefully designed by the Framers."[50] Powell emphasized, "The Framers believed that the separate sphere of sovereignty reserved to the States would serve as an effective 'counterpoise' to the power of the Federal Government."[51] But "federal overreaching under the Commerce Clause undermines the constitutionally mandated balance of powers between the States and the Federal Government, *a balance designed to protect our fundamental liberties.*"[52] As Powell concluded, the effect of eviscerating structural limits on national power meant that "federal political officials, invoking the Commerce Clause, are the sole judges of the limits of their own power," a result "inconsistent with the fundamental principles of our constitutional system."[53]

Justice Rehnquist, who dissented separately in *Garcia*, promised that the rule of *National League of Cities* "will, I am confident, in time command the support of a majority of this Court."[54] And indeed, although *Garcia* has not yet been explicitly overruled, the conservatives have prevailed on a number of occasions, often laudably reining in national government power on federalism grounds.[55] In particular, the Court under Chief Justice Rehnquist has concluded that the national government's power to regulate commerce—which was invoked during the New Deal and Great Society as the constitutional basis for sweeping regulatory enactments related tangentially at best to interstate commerce—is not without boundaries.[56] In the 1995 decision in *United States v. Lopez*,[57] the Court struck down for the first time since the New Deal a law predicated on the Commerce Clause: the Gun-Free School Zones Act, which prohibited possession of a firearm within 500 feet of a school. Five years later, in *United States v. Morrison*,[58] the Court invalidated a civil remedy provision of the Violence Against Women Act. Both decisions were 5-4, with Chief Justice Rehnquist and Justices Sandra Day O'Connor, Antonin Scalia, Anthony Kennedy, and Clarence Thomas forming the majority.

In *Lopez*, the Court recognized that the "few and defined" powers of the national government were meant to "ensure protection of our fundamental liberties"; and that the purpose of a "healthy balance of power between the States and the Federal Government" is to "reduce the risk of tyranny and abuse from either front."[59] In more narrowly construing the national government's power to regulate commerce, the Court noted that in order for Congress to possess authority, the nature of its act must actually affect commerce in a substantial manner.[60] The fiction that had been invented by liberal activists that *everything* affects interstate commerce sufficiently to trigger congressional regulatory authority under the Commerce Clause was at last repudiated (albeit by a single vote) in a victory for the true principles of federalism.

The Court also clipped Congress's wings with regard to its enforcement authority under the 14th Amendment. Following a narrow interpretation by the Supreme Court of the First Amendment's guarantee of free exercise of religion,[61] the Court in *City of Boerne v. Flores*[62] struck down the Religious Freedom Restoration Act, which was designed to restore the lost protections. The Court held that Congress's enforcement power under the 14th Amendment was purely "remedial" and "preventative," rather than "substantive" in the sense of defining or creating rights.[63] The decision was something of a mixed bag from a federalism standpoint: It held Congress to its defined powers, but those powers in that instance were exercised in a manner intended to expand liberty. In the long run, *City of Boerne* likely will exert a pro-freedom influence by curbing congressional power to create entitlements.

Additionally, the Court has acted to limit the scope of *Garcia*. In *New York v. United States*,[64] the Court took on the common congressional practice of making federal funding contingent upon states taking certain desired actions. In striking one provision of a radioactive waste law, the Court concluded that under the Tenth Amendment, such choices must be truly voluntary. As Justice O'Connor declared, "A choice between two unconstitutionally coercive regulatory techniques is no choice at all."[65] The Court's majority established that "Congress may not simply 'commandee[r] the legislative processes of states by directly compelling them to enact and enforce a federal regulatory program.'"[66] The Court subsequently invoked the "anti-commandeering" principle by striking down a provision in the Brady Act that required state law-enforcement officials to conduct background checks for gun owners, holding that under the Tenth Amendment, Congress cannot compel "ministerial" acts by state governments.[67]

In sum, recent jurisprudence has advanced the goals of federalism by limiting the powers of Congress, as they directly regulate both the states and the conduct of individuals. But what about the flip side of federalism, in which federal courts are entrusted with the duty under the 14th Amendment to defend federal constitutional rights against violations by state and local governments? Here, sadly, the record is much more mixed—as the subsequent chapters will illustrate—and depends largely on which types of rights are involved. Conservatives generally are more vigilant in protecting individuals against racial preferences and abuses of private-property rights, liberals more trustworthy when it comes to protecting privacy and the rights of criminal defendants, and ideological lines are blurry on free-speech issues. Again, much of this inconsistency emanates from confusion over the proper meaning and role of federalism.

A classic clash along those lines involved the application of federal antitrust laws to limit the anticompetitive actions of local governments (states have long been exempted from antitrust laws). In many instances, local government regulations directly and substantially affect interstate commerce; and unlike the monopolistic acts of private entities, the market often cannot overcome the rules set by government. That would seem to warrant congressional intervention to limit the anticompetitive actions of local governments under both the Commerce Clause and, arguably, the 14th Amendment.

In a pair of decisions in the late 1970s and early '80s, the Supreme Court applied the antitrust laws to curb such abuses by local government.[68] In dissent to *Lafayette*, Justice Potter Stewart complained of the intolerable threat of liability, for local governments "often take actions that might violate the antitrust laws if taken by private persons, such as granting exclusive franchises, enacting restrictive zoning ordinances, and providing public services on a monopoly basis."[69] Exactly! That time, in his majority opinion, Justice Brennan—ordinarily no friend of free markets but a strong advocate of national regulatory power—weighed in with incisive analysis, declaring that local governments

> participate in and affect the economic life of this Nation in a great number and variety of ways. . . . [T]hey are fully capable of aggrandizing other economic units with which they interrelate, with the potential of serious distortion of the rational and efficient allocation of resources, and the efficiency of free markets which the regime of competition embodied in the antitrust laws is thought to engender. If municipalities were free to make economic choices counseled solely by their own parochial interests and without

regard to their anticompetitive effects, a serious chink in the armor of antitrust protection would be introduced at odds with the comprehensive national policy Congress established.[70]

The Supreme Court decisions touched off a bitter struggle within the Reagan administration between states' rights conservatives and free market advocates, which brought to the surface the broader battle among conservatives over the principles of federalism. Unfortunately, the states' rights crowd prevailed, and President Reagan signed legislation in 1984 sharply reducing antitrust liability for local governments, thereby removing a weapon against grassroots tyranny.[71]

Two recent cases in particular illustrate the shifting perspectives on federalism and the ends-justify-the-means approach of liberals and conservatives toward issues of individual rights and state autonomy. In its 1996 decision in *Romer v. Evans*, a majority of the Supreme Court invalidated, under the equal protection guarantee of the 14th Amendment, a ballot initiative that amended the Colorado Constitution to prohibit local governments from enacting laws forbidding discrimination against homosexuals. In a 6-3 decision authored by Justice Kennedy,[72] the Court found that the provision singled out homosexuals as "a solitary class with respect to transactions and relations in both the private and governmental spheres."[73] That created a "special disability," wherein homosexuals alone could not seek protection against discrimination through ordinary democratic processes but instead would have to secure a new constitutional amendment.[74] Declaring that the guarantee of equal protection states "a commitment to the law's neutrality where the rights of persons are at stake,"[75] the Court held that a state "cannot so deem a class of persons a stranger to its laws,"[76] and struck down the provision.

Not surprisingly, the dissenters—Chief Justice Rehnquist and Justices Scalia and Thomas—objected strongly on federalism grounds. Characterizing the issue as a debate over cultural norms, Justice Scalia argued, "Since the Constitution of the United States says nothing about this subject, it is left to be resolved by normal democratic means, including the democratic adoption of provisions in state constitutions."[77] Declaring that the right as articulated by the majority "has no foundation in American constitutional law,"[78] Scalia concluded that the Court had "invent[ed] a novel and extravagant constitutional doctrine to take the victory away from traditional forces" of majority rule.[79]

The Court's lineup in *Romer v. Evans* was unsurprising—the Court's liberals and moderates joining together to apply federal constitutional protections to prevent abuses by a state, and the conservatives voting to preserve state prerogatives and majority rule. So when similar equal protection issues were presented to the Court four years later in the midst of a bitter presidential election struggle, one might have predicted a similar outcome.[80] Indeed, the outcome *was* similar—the Supreme Court intervened and overturned local election processes—but seven of the nine justices had switched sides.

In *Bush v. Gore*, the five-member Court majority (Chief Justice Rehnquist and Justices O'Connor, Scalia, Kennedy, and Thomas) anchored its decision in the fundamental right that encompasses "equal weight accorded to each vote and the equal dignity owed to each voter."[81] Recognizing their vulnerability to attacks on federalism grounds, the majority admonished, "[n]one are more conscious of the vital limits on judicial authority than are the members of this Court, and none stand more in admiration of the Constitution's design to leave the selection of the President to the People, through their legislatures, and to the political sphere."[82] Indeed, in a concurring opinion, Chief Justice Rehnquist acknowledged that "[i]n most cases, comity and respect for federalism compel us to defer to the decisions of state courts on issues of state law. That practice reflects our understanding that the decisions of state courts are definitive pronouncements of the will of the States as sovereigns."[83] However, the Court found, "we are presented with a situation where a state court with the power to assure uniformity has ordered a statewide recount with minimal procedural safeguards,"[84] and it halted the recount ordered by the Florida Supreme Court.

This time, the liberal dissenters—Justices John Paul Stevens, David Souter, Ruth Bader Ginsburg, and Stephen Breyer—wielded the sword of states' rights. Declaring the decision a "federal assault on the Florida election procedures,"[85] they asserted that the Constitution's provisions regarding national elections "can hardly be read to invite this Court to disrupt a State's republican regime."[86] To the contrary, Justice Ginsburg declared, "Federal courts defer to state high courts' interpretations of their state's own law. This principle reflects the core of federalism, on which all agree."[87]

The lesson arising from the inconsistent perspectives in those cases is that we are all federalists now, except when we are not. It is difficult to find anyone, other than the swing justices, O'Connor and Kennedy, who agrees with both *Romer* and *Bush*, or who disagrees with both. And surely, there are jurisprudential grounds other than the policy preferences of the particular justices to justify the divergent votes. But the apparent flip-flop, at least in terms of rhetoric, by both liberal and conservative justices, underscores the current ad hoc state of federalism jurisprudence practiced by both sides of the ideological divide.

That is not to say that the current Court has not scored some important advances for true federalism, particularly in applying principles of federalism to restrain the reach and power of the national government. But because it has lost its grasp on the core values underlying federalism, too often the Court has allowed the doctrine to shield rather than root out abuses of individual rights. "Today's Court has lost sight of the People," charges Akhil Amar, "and so it has transmogrified doctrines of federalism and sovereignty into their very antitheses."[88]

It is not only the Supreme Court justices who are inconsistent about federalism, but activists on both sides of the ideological divide as well. Many liberals love to eviscerate state autonomy when they propose all manner of federal mandates, from wage and hour laws to education to environmental regulations to government-run health care. Conservatives often resist such incursions on states'-rights grounds. But turn the tables and the positions switch. When the Massachusetts Supreme Judicial Court decided to interpret its constitution to allow same-sex marriage, many social conservatives responded with a proposed constitutional amendment to forbid that exercise of state sovereignty. The decision and the response by some social conservatives allowed liberal constitutional scholar Cass Sunstein to characterize the Massachusetts decision as "a remarkable tribute to U.S. federalism."[89] Indeed, it is difficult to square the argument by social conservatives in the abortion context that states should have the power to define life, with the view that states should not be able to define marriage.

This is not to suggest any particular position on the merits of the underlying issues, but rather to puzzle over the maddening inconsistency with which advocates across the ideological spectrum invoke the mantle of federalism and just as easily jettison it when the mood strikes. Such constitutional relativism erodes the integrity of federalism and its value in protecting precious freedoms.

As envisioned by the framers of the original constitution and perfected by the authors of the 14th Amendment, the framework for federalism is fairly simple and straightforward. The Constitution creates a national government of strictly defined and limited powers, and expresses a judicially enforceable preference for the decentralization of decision making, ultimately resting sovereignty with each individual. However, in order to protect individual liberty, the Constitution invests both the national and state governments with the power to curb violations of those rights by one another. Hence, there is no ultimate preference for either national or state power. Rather, the goal of federalism is to secure individual liberty.

The failure of American jurisprudence to remain faithful to the principles of federalism has led, painfully and predictably, to an erosion of freedom. The notion of federalism as a mere "truism" has abetted a sweeping expansion of the powers of national government, an expansion that has been widely documented. Meanwhile, the notion of federalism as a justification for unfettered "states' rights" has given rein to a phenomenon that is less remarked upon: the explosive growth of state and local government and the resulting epidemic of grassroots tyranny.

Grassroots tyranny—the violation of the fundamental rights of individuals by their own local governments, often unremedied by state or federal courts—takes many forms. It is to the documentation of some of the many manifestations of grassroots tyranny that the next several chapters are devoted.

PART TWO

The Erosion of Liberty

In this part, I set forth a number of examples of abuses of rights inflicted by state and local governments upon their residents (or, in some instances, upon residents of other states). Within the areas I have selected, these examples barely scratch the surface; and I have not covered entire categories, such as police brutality, abuses of taxpayer rights, and interference with religious liberty. The purpose of these examples is to illustrate some of the many manifestations of grassroots tyranny that deeply and adversely affect the real lives of real people. Many of them are somewhat aberrational because they have happy endings, either due to extensive media coverage or successful legal challenges. Most people who fight city hall toil in obscurity and lack the resources to overcome the often overwhelming odds and reach a successful outcome.

Not all readers will agree that all of the examples constitute abuses of individual rights; but I am confident that nearly every reader will see much that is troublesome and outside the bounds of appropriate government power.

4

Freedom of Commerce and Enterprise

It is quite common in these later days for certain classes of citizens—those engaged in this or that business—to appeal to the government—national, state, or municipal—to aid them by legislation against another class of citizens engaged in the same business, but in some other way. This class legislation, when indulged in, seldom benefits the general public, but nearly always aids the few for whose benefit it is enacted, not only at the expense of the few against whom it is ostensibly directed, but also at the expense and to the detriment of the many, for whose benefit all legislation should be, in a republican form of government, framed and devised. This kind of legislation should receive no encouragement at the hands of the courts.
— Michigan Supreme Court, 1889[1]

IF THERE WERE ever a nostalgic television show about small-town America, Garland Allen would be the barber. For decades, the elderly black practitioner has been cutting hair in rural Lebanon, Tennessee, in a barbershop that draws old-timers to play a game of pool, get a haircut and a shoeshine, and swap stories. Allen has worked in the shop since he was a young boy, when he learned to cut hair at his father's side.

In July 1996, however, Garland Allen was arrested in his shop. His crime: "impersonating a professional," a felony under Tennessee law punishable by up to six years in prison.

Allen was "impersonating a professional" not because he had caused harm to anyone but because he lacked a barbering

license from the state of Tennessee. No one, including the
Tennessee Board of Barbering Examiners or the rival barber
who turned him in, claimed that Allen was unqualified.
Rather, he lacked the requisite license, and that was enough
to get him arrested.

When Allen was a young man, there were no Tennessee
barber colleges that admitted blacks, so he learned to cut hair
informally but professionally. As an adult, Allen could not
afford the nine months or five thousand dollars necessary to
go to school or get his license. So, for the heinous crime of
lacking a license, Allen was arrested.

The ordeal attracted attention throughout the state as well
as the threat of a lawsuit from the Institute for Justice. Happily, the state backed down and allowed Garland Allen to continue practicing his craft. The spectacle of a man faced with
prison merely for earning an honest living in a profession he
had engaged in for decades seemed decidedly un-American.
But unfortunately, barriers to enterprise erected by state and
local governments are all too common today in a nation doc-
trinally committed to opportunity.

The Statue of Liberty is one of the most resonant symbols
of the American experiment. For generations, it has stood as
a beacon to millions of oppressed people around the world,
many of whom sought political freedom, but many more of
whom sought economic opportunity.

Freedom of enterprise is a fundamental right that most
Americans believe they possess, yet in reality it receives
almost no legal protection at all. It is a sobering commentary
on our constitutional evolution that if the government tries to
take away someone's welfare check, the taxpayer-financed
Legal Services Corporation will come to the rescue and tie it
up in knots; but if government decides to arbitrarily limit

access to a business or profession, even for the benefit of sheltered special interests, it may do so with impunity.

Two California entrepreneurs could be excused for think-
ing that not only the symbolism but the tangible promise of
opportunity has tarnished a bit. Joanne Cornwell is the chair-
person of the African Studies Department at San Diego State
University. But she also created a hairstyling technique that
she patented as "Sisterlocks." It is a highly intricate style that
requires specialized training and tools to perform and several
hours to complete for each client. Dr. Cornwell opened a
salon in her own home, and the style became very popular.
Meanwhile, she compiled a training program and franchised
Sisterlocks to dozens of other stylists. Her business model
created lucrative opportunities for herself and her franchisees, while providing a popular service that drew upon traditional African culture and hairstyles.

At the same time, Ali Rasheed and his African-born wife,
Assiyah, were operating a salon in San Diego called The Braiderie. There several stylists, mostly African immigrants,
engaged in hair braiding and other traditional styles that trace
their African roots thousands of years. But The Braiderie was
slapped with a citation from the California State Board of Barbering and Cosmetology on the grounds that the business was
not a licensed cosmetology salon and the braiders were not
licensed cosmetologists. Dr. Cornwell likewise was operating
without a license, and therefore outside the law.[2]

At the time, California required 1,600 hours of prescribed
training for anyone engaged in cosmetology—substantially
more than the training required for an emergency medical
technician or a police officer. As Taalib-din Uqdah, president
of the American Hairbraiding and Natural Haircare Association exclaimed, "We're braiding hair, not practicing brain
surgery!" Almost none of the curriculum related in the

slightest to African hairstyling. About half of the required training dealt with the use of chemicals in the hair. But African hairstylists militantly believe that chemicals have destroyed black hair and are used primarily to alter its natural state, and they never use chemicals. Furthermore, cosmetologists are required to learn about white hairstyles that haven't been popular in decades, along with fingernail-painting and the use of cosmetics—services that African hairstylists do not provide. The training must take place in a licensed school, which costs several thousand dollars and takes nearly a year to complete. After the training, cosmetologists must pass an examination demonstrating mastery of knowledge that is irrelevant or antithetical to African hairstyling; as well as techniques that, if applied to a black subject, require the straightening of hair, something that an African hairstylist would never do. About the only hairstyling skill that a would-be cosmetologist does not have to learn anything about or demonstrate any proficiency in performing is—you guessed it—African hairstyling. Anyone purporting to teach African styling would have to qualify for a separate instructor's license, which requires even more of the same. Few traditionally licensed cosmetology instructors know much if anything about the specialized art of hair braiding; yet they possess exclusive jurisdiction to "train" even those who have been braiding for decades.

Until recently, rules of that type predominated in all 50 states and the District of Columbia, turning aspiring entrepreneurs like Joanne Cornwell and Ali Rasheed into outlaws. The rules typically are enforced by licensing boards composed primarily of members of the regulated profession, who of course have a vested interest in stifling competition from newcomers. Most hair braiders in such states operate underground—thereby depriving the stylists of opportunities to operate openly in the mainstream economy, while preventing law-enforcement officials from enforcing valid health and safety regulations and destroying precious employment opportunities for people with few skills.

The regime makes little sense from the standpoint of entrepreneurs, stylists, consumers, or even the government; but the regulations, like many others, are kept in place by the regulated industry as a means of sheltering it from competition. Represented by the Institute for Justice, Cornwell and Rasheed took the Board of Barbering and Cosmetology to federal court—and won.[3] Fortunately, instead of appealing, the state deregulated African hairstyling, requiring only the completion of courses in hygiene, sanitation, and public safety. Cornwell, Rasheed, and thousands of other African hairstylists now can operate flourishing enterprises in the light of day. But similar laws remain on the books in dozens of other states, needlessly thwarting economic opportunities, primarily in the inner city.

Through a series of studies on state and local regulatory barriers to entrepreneurship,[4] my colleagues and I have documented myriad state and local regulations that stymie boot-straps capitalism—the opportunity for people with good ideas but little capital or formal training to begin climbing the rungs of the economic ladder. Government regulates everything from home-based businesses to day-care centers to alternative transit systems—the type of infrastructure occupations that could offer abundant entrepreneurial and employment opportunities to people of modest means. The sheer bureaucracy that awaits anyone wanting to open a business—from business licenses to zoning permits—can defeat enterprising individuals before they even start their businesses. The rules often force aspiring entrepreneurs into illegal occupations—the captains of industry in the inner city are often drug merchants—or into the black market, where their access to capital and governments' ability to regulate or tax them are nonexistent.

In all, at least 500 occupations, representing 10 percent of all professions, require government licenses, often conferred by boards composed of members of the regulated profession, invested with the coercive power to limit entry and competition.[5] Additionally, entry into many businesses, such as residential trash collection and taxicabs, is limited by local government, often for the purpose of protecting monopolies or oligopolies. Such restrictions, declares economist Walter Williams, "discriminate against certain people," particularly "outsiders, latecomers, and [the] resourceless," among whom members of minority groups "are disproportionately represented."[6] For many who fervently desire the path of self-help, pursuit of the American Dream has become a nightmare.[7]

And law provides little respite. Despite the fact that economic liberty—the right to pursue a business or profession free from arbitrary or excessive government regulation—was one of the foremost rights intended to be protected among the "privileges or immunities" of citizens under the 14th Amendment, federal courts traditionally have provided little refuge, even if the government wipes an entire industry out of existence for apparently protectionist purposes.[8] The courts apply the misnamed "rational basis" test, which requires neither that the government articulate a basis for regulation nor that it be rational. Rather, the courts will infer a rational basis for economic regulation, even if it did not motivate the legislature's actions.[9]

One industry in which entry-level entrepreneurial opportunities are thwarted by protectionist government regulation is transportation. In the early part of the 20th century, "jitneys" provided the principal form of public transportation in

American cities. Jitneys were privately owned vehicles that would transport passengers anywhere along a fixed route for a flat fee. But when streetcars came into existence, the streetcar industry went from city to city enacting anti-jitney ordinances that wiped out the competition, not through market competition but by government fiat.

Today, the streetcars are long gone, but the laws against commuter vans—the modern-day successors to jitneys—remain on the local books, supported by heavily subsidized, unionized, and often inefficient government bus monopolies. (By contrast, commuter vans often efficiently provide airport transportation services because they are regulated by states or airport authorities rather than cities.)

In Jamaica, Queens, however, thousands of mostly illegal commuter vans operate, providing a highly personalized and inexpensive alternative to the public bus monopoly. The vans are vital to the heavily immigrant working-class community because they not only take people to work, they also put people to work. The city forbids transit alternatives on streets that are bus routes—which is pretty much every public thoroughfare in New York City. The police constantly ticket and harass the van drivers, even though the city anxiously turns to the vans to fill in for its public-transit system every time the bus drivers go on strike.

Two van owners, Vincent Cummins and Hector Ricketts, challenged the law in a suit filed by the Institute for Justice, and were supported by a second lawsuit filed by then-mayor Rudy Giuliani. In 1999, a state judge stripped the city council—which was heavily influenced by and responsive to the public transit union—of its power to control van licenses.[10] The ruling removed some of the barriers that limited entry into the van business, but other restrictions remain—as they do in many other cities, arbitrarily limiting entrepreneurial opportunities and highly desired consumer options while forcing taxpayers to subsidize bloated, monopolistic transit systems.

In most cities, the one relatively unregulated transit service (again, because they typically are regulated by states rather than cities) are private limousine services. They are usually forbidden from picking up hailing passengers, but are available for prearranged transportation. But not in Las Vegas, where the limousine industry is largely controlled by a handful of politically powerful companies. Independent limousine drivers were required by state law to secure a certificate of public convenience and necessity, and existing companies were allowed to intervene in opposition to their applications. The oligopolists' legal demands upon applicants were so onerous that they usually bled the newcomers financially dry before the process was even completed. The standard in Nevada required demonstration that the new business would not adversely affect existing businesses—again, an absurd and impossible standard to meet.[11] Again, an Institute for Justice lawsuit was largely successful in removing regulatory barriers, with a state court ruling in 2001 that the regime "amounted to an onerous and unduly burdensome process,"[12] but not before several independent limousine operators went out of business.

State and local governments impede access to other entry-level businesses as well. In several states, the government forbids the direct sale of caskets to consumers. In Tennessee, the Rev. Nathaniel Craigmiles was tired of his parishioners having to pay exorbitant prices to funeral homes for caskets, so he started his own storefront casket business. But the store was shut down by state regulators, because state law required anyone selling caskets to hold a funeral manager license. The license required extensive training in embalming and other activities totally unrelated to selling caskets. The regulations were supported, naturally, by the funeral home industry, which extracts huge monopoly profits from the sale of caskets to grieving families.

The state defended the law on, among other grounds, the unproven contention that leakage from caskets could cause public health or safety problems. But in Tennessee, the law does not even require burial in caskets at all. Again, the Institute for Justice filed suit. Finding the law palpably irrational, both the federal district court[13] and the U.S. Court of Appeals for the Sixth Circuit struck down the law[14] — though an Oklahoma district court upheld a similar law, which is now pending on appeal in the Tenth Circuit.[15]

While advocates of economic liberty were battling casket monopolists in Tennessee and Oklahoma, a similar fight was raging in Seattle, over trash. The java-loving city's official website boasts, "Welcome to Seattle, an excellent place for business." But despite its liberal reputation, the city's policies often promote big business to the detriment of free enterprise.

That predilection was evident in 2003 when the city council voted on a "housekeeping" measure, acting to change the definition of municipal waste to include waste generated by construction, demolition, and land-clearing. The subtle change had the effect of expanding the scope of the city's waste-collection contract with two garbage-hauling behemoths, Waste Management and Allied Waste/Robanco, so that they now had a monopoly on the hauling of construction waste that previously they were forced to share in an open market with a number of small haulers. "Overnight, the small haulers were put out of business," reported *Seattle Post-Intelligencer* columnist Chi-Dooh Li. "Their way of earning a living, honorable and useful one day, became a criminal offense the next day."[16]

Many cities confer monopolies for collection of residential or commercial trash. The rationale is that having several competing firms operate on overlapping routes causes congestion and inefficiencies. Such logic precludes competition in most of the trash-hauling business. But whatever the logic for monopolies in that context, it doesn't extend to the hauling of construction waste, which takes place strictly on an on-call basis. The only reason for putting construction waste within the trash-hauling monopoly was to benefit the monopolists — not to advance environmental objectives or create economies of scale. My colleague Bill Mauer, executive director of the Institute for Justice Washington Chapter, pointed out that "the same construction waste ends up in the same transfer station. The only difference is with a monopoly, there are no choices for consumers and no opportunities for would-be entrepreneurs."[17]

Recognizing the economic insanity of its own rules, the city exempted its own construction waste from the monopoly.[18] Instead, it only forbade private developers from hiring independent contractors. Joe Ventenbergs, owner of Kendall Trucking, voiced fear that the monopoly would drive his small company, into which he had invested his life savings, out of business. One of his customers, developer Ron Haider, complained that the law prevented him from patronizing Ventenbergs's company, which he preferred over the monopolists' because of its lower prices and more reliable service. The two business owners joined in a lawsuit arguing that the monopoly violated their constitutional rights.[19] Unless David can prevail over Goliath in this case and others like it, cities like Seattle will be able to continue to destroy businesses with impunity for no better purpose than economic protectionism.

In our free society, consumer choice should be the rule, not the object of governmental disdain and displacement. With the advent of the Internet, consumer choices are more abundant than ever before. But the process of disintermediation—the elimination of the middleman—threatens existing economic interests, leading businesses to turn to the state's regulatory power to seek protectionist shelter from competition. As a result, from the sale of contact lenses to automobiles to insurance, state laws often frustrate the vast commercial potential of the Internet. That is especially anomalous given that the original constitution was enacted in large measure to eliminate and prevent parochial trade barriers and to guarantee free trade among the states.

Juanita Swedenburg is the owner of a small winery in Middleburg, Virginia. As is the case with many small wineries, most of her sales are to visitors to the winery or to those attracted by word of mouth. But when customers from out of state ask her to ship wine to their homes, Swedenburg tells them she can't. Most states declare such shipping a criminal misdemeanor, and if Swedenburg were to ship wine to Florida, Maryland, or Utah, she would be committing a felony.

All told, about half the states prohibit the direct interstate sale and shipment of wine to consumers. Many of the same states permit direct shipping by their own wineries. The purpose of the restrictions is to protect the monopoly profits—often amounting to a third of the price of a bottle of wine—of liquor distributors, who tenaciously defend the laws. Over the past few decades, the number of American wineries has grown exponentially, and the overwhelming majority are small, family-owned enterprises with small distribution. At the same time, the wholesaler industry has experienced severe consolidation. That has created an economic mismatch, with thousands of wines produced that cannot find a place within limited distributor inventories or on store shelves. The result: Wineries are deprived of market access, consumers are deprived of otherwise readily available choices, prices are artificially higher, and states are deprived of potential new tax revenues.[20] But the multibillion-dollar liquor distributor oligopolists are fat and happy.

The Institute for Justice and others have filed lawsuits challenging the protectionist bans on direct interstate wine shipping. Thus far, bans have been struck down in Virginia, North Carolina, Texas, and Michigan as violations of the Constitution's commerce clause, but upheld in Indiana and New York as valid exercises of the states' regulatory power over alcohol under the 21st Amendment.[21] The U.S. Supreme Court accepted review of Juanita Swedenburg's case and a companion case in spring 2004, and a ruling is expected by summer 2005. If the Supreme Court remains true to the core promise of free trade among the states, its ruling will help vindicate the great promise of consumer freedom in the Internet age. If not, a new era of government-sanctioned economic protectionism will dim that potential.

The lesson that traditional avenues of entrepreneurship are steadily being choked off by oppressive government intrusion is trickling down even to young people. As I was growing up, paper routes, lemonade stands, and even selling eggs from my Easter basket were mainstays of my disposable income.

Following recently in that great American tradition was a high school student from Tempe, Arizona, named Christian Alf. The Phoenix area is infested with roof rats, which eat fruit from trees and often enter homes through chimneys and other openings. First as a favor to friends, then as a lucrative part-time enterprise, Alf began covering such openings with wire mesh to prevent rodent intrusion. He provided this service for $30, while pest control companies charged ten times that amount.

Then the Arizona Structural Pest Control Commission stepped in. The boy was engaged in pest control without a license, the commission charged, and it ordered Alf to stop. He did.

A public outcry ensued, and the Institute for Justice Arizona Chapter threatened to sue. The commission backed down, and Alf went back to work. As the *East Valley Tribune* editorialized, "Alf now has a whole new dimension opening up for his future. At first all he wanted to be is an aerospace engineer. Thanks to this experience with our on-the-ball government, he's becoming something far more important: A civil libertarian."[22] The whole story goes to show that sometimes the worst type of rat is a bureaucrat.

Myriad regulations also thwart opportunities for home-based businesses, whose potential also has expanded in the Internet era. Home-based businesses provide an especially good outlet for stay-at-home parents to earn income while caring for their children. But zoning and other regulations often impede that potential and turn legitimate small businesspeople into outlaws.

I encountered two extremely unlikely outlaws when I was researching for my study on barriers to entrepreneurship in Charlotte, North Carolina. Two elderly women, Mrs. Connell and Mrs. Koller, were crocheting pillows and canning preserves in their homes for sale at the local farmers' market. The local zoning administrator advised them that their activities were illegal because a city zoning ordinance forbade the manufacture of goods for sale within a home.

Incredulous that the city would construe such a law against those ladies, I wrote to the zoning administrator asking him to tell me that it wasn't so. No response. I wrote him a second time, this time threatening a lawsuit. No response. I wrote a third letter, this time announcing the date the lawsuit would be filed and copying the city attorney. Within days, I received a letter from the city attorney assuring me that the zoning ordinance would certainly not apply to pillows and preserves. Mrs. Connell and Mrs. Koller could operate freely in society again.

Over the brief course of the controversy, I knew my clients only by their surnames. Only when I subsequently received a sweet thank-you note did I realize that their first names, appropriately enough for the rebels they had become, were Thelma and Louise.

Fortunately Thelma and Louise didn't have to go to the same lengths as the movie characters to protect their dignity. But others do. Few start-up entrepreneurs have the money, time, or sophistication to fight city hall. When they try, they find the odds overwhelmingly against them. And despite some optimistic recent victories, the courts remain generally hostile forums in which to present economic-liberty claims. The plethora of laws that stifle economic opportunity make a mockery of our nation's promise of opportunity.

Still, freedom of enterprise is one of the most profoundly shared values that bring Americans together. With Americans united in common cause behind the courageous determination of aspiring entrepreneurs, we can restore economic liberty as a fundamental civil right. As Hector Ricketts proclaimed when he won the right to operate his van service, "Even in New York City it's possible for little people to have their concerns addressed. People in other cities should try this."[23]

He's right. Economic liberty might just prove contagious.

5

Private-
Property
Rights

How could . . . the government . . . have the nerve to come
and take away from the poor working people and give it
to the rich? . . . They say, "I demand, you going to be moving, you like it or not." What right do you have if you let
them do what they want? The American people don't got
no rights.
    —Mary Ann Pillow, featured on KAET *Horizon*

This is my home. It's been my home for 36 years. If I
move, it won't be a home. It'll just be a house I'm living
in. And I don't think I'd ever get to a place where I could
ever call that home.
                                        —Kenneth Pillow

IN MARCH 2003, the *New York Times* reported the sad plight of
farmers in Communist China whose land was being taken by
the government to build factories. Song Defu heard about it
the previous May, when his cornstalks were reaching for the
sky. The television news reported that farming no longer
would be allowed in his town, and that 500 farmers would be
displaced in favor of an industrial park. A few days later the
bulldozers came and the fields were plowed under—despite a
provision in the Chinese Constitution providing that local vil-
lages "must not illegally alter or annul contracts," including
land leases. The village leader swears it was all by the book.
"All the proper procedures were carried out," he declared.

"[T]here are always a minority who are unhappy." The human consequences were devastating. "Farmers who have lost their land, yes, they find work," another villager remarked, "but it's often just picking and selling old garbage in Beijing."[1]

Just business as usual in a totalitarian state where property rights are not recognized. Such a scenario could never take place in a free society committed to private-property rights like America, right? After all, the U.S. Constitution expressly limits the exercise of eminent domain—the right of a government to take property—to instances of "public use," and only when "just compensation" is made. Public use typically entails the construction of schools, roads, or the like. Unfortunately, excesses in the use of this carefully bounded power play out every day in cities across the nation.

Randy Bailey owns a brake shop on the corner of Country Club Drive and Main Street, a major intersection in Mesa, Arizona. For more than 20 years, Randy and his father before him have installed brakes that stop cars on a dime. Randy hopes one day to hand the shop down to his son. The shop does a good business, and it is emphatically not for sale.

But these days, that doesn't matter, because cities view all property as up for grabs.[2] Eminent domain is one of the most destructive powers of government, and historically it has been used only for public purposes such as roads, schools, and hospitals. But increasingly, it is abused to serve private ends that happen to coincide with the government's policy objectives. If a city views a property as underutilized—that is, if it might produce more tax revenue or generate more jobs in someone else's hands—city officials may exercise the power of eminent domain to take it from the current owner and give it to someone they like better.

If that sounds more like socialism than a nation grounded in a belief in the sanctity of private-property rights, that's because it is. But it's socialism of the most perverse kind, a sort of Robin Hood in reverse, whereby property is taken from poor and working-class people and given to wealthy, politically connected people or corporations. In most instances, it's corporate welfare of the most naked kind. Most people have no idea that the phenomenon of eminent domain abuse exists at all—or that it could happen in America—until it happens to them.

Randy Bailey learned that painful lesson when he started hearing rumors that Ken Lenhart, the owner of an Ace Hardware store, wanted to expand and relocate to the very corner occupied by Bailey's Brake Service and his neighbors—a Maaco auto body shop, a restaurant, and several homes and other businesses. Lenhart started buying up some properties, often tearing down the existing structures and leaving the wreckage on the lot. Lenhart contacted the city and asked it to assemble the other properties so he could purchase the entire corner.

The city obliged, designating the corner part of a "redevelopment" zone. Never fear, the city advised the property owners: We promise you'll be fairly compensated. But several owners, including Bailey, didn't want to leave. Bailey wanted to remain at his location for precisely the reason Lenhart coveted it: It is the prime commercial intersection in Mesa. Moreover, all of his customers knew that's where he was located.

Growing alarmed, Bailey contacted Lenhart and asked him to make Bailey's Brake Service part of the project. Don't talk to me, Lenhart responded, talk to the city.

The city took bids to redevelop the corner, drawing its specifications to match Lenhart's desires. Not surprisingly, Lenhart won the bid. Not only would the city condemn all the property he wanted to acquire and sell it to him at below-market prices, it would throw in a two-million-dollar subsidy to boot. The city told Bailey and his neighbors that they could negotiate over price, but not the right to stay.

As properties around his shop were being bulldozed, Bailey fought back. Represented by the Institute for Justice, he filed an opposition to the eminent domain action arguing that it violated the Arizona Constitution's guarantee that "private property shall not be taken for private use." The city argued that "public use" really meant "public benefit," and that the city's determination of public benefit was dispositive. The city repeatedly increased its cash offers, asserting publicly that Bailey was really interested only in more money. The bureaucrats simply could not grasp the concept that Bailey actually didn't want to sell at any price.

Bailey lost the opening round in trial court, but the court granted an injunction halting the bulldozers. As the case went to appeal, Bailey's cause was backed by the *East Valley Tribune*, *Arizona Republic*, and even a segment on *60 Minutes*. Finally the Court of Appeals struck down the condemnation because its principal beneficiaries were private.[3] Randy Bailey had vindicated his property rights—but only after several years of constant anxiety to win a battle he should never have had to fight.

Randy Bailey's case reveals only the tip of the confiscatory iceberg. In a 2003 report entitled *Public Power, Private Gain*,[4] my colleague Dana Berliner compiled more than ten thousand cases over a five-year period in which the eminent domain power was threatened or used to take private property from one private owner to transfer it to another.* Because no central database exists, these only comprised the cases that

*Eminent domain abuse is not just an American phenomenon. A delightful Australian movie, *The Castle* (available in many video stores), depicts a working-class family's poignant battle to save their home from government confiscation. I recommend it highly.

she was able to actually document, leading her to conclude that they represent only a fraction of the actual number. Among the states with high numbers of eminent domain abuses were California, Kansas, Michigan, Maryland, Ohio, Pennsylvania, Florida, and New Jersey.[5] New York, Missouri, and Kansas have the weakest legal safeguards against eminent domain abuse.

New York may be the most flagrant abuser of its eminent domain power. Between 1998 and 2002, it condemned small businesses for the New York Stock Exchange, the New York Times Company, Costco, and Stop & Shop. An inner-city church was taken for commercial development, while a family furniture-building business in East Harlem was taken for a Home Depot. Protections against eminent domain abuse in New York are virtually nonexistent. All a condemning authority has to do is publish a small advertisement in the legal notices section of the local newspaper. It does not have to state the consequences of the owners' failure to act. Yet if the owners happen not to see the notice, or to act promptly, they will lose their right to challenge the taking on public-use grounds 30 days following publication.[6]

Even in jurisdictions with rules less draconian than New York, the odds are stacked heavily against property owners who want to keep their homes and businesses. The concepts of negotiation and voluntary sale are a cruel joke. Typically, the government will make an offer for property it desires, and if the owner declines, it can secure from a local court an "order of immediate possession," transferring ownership to the government. Then the bulldozers move in. Few property owners have the money to hire a lawyer in an uphill battle to establish that the proposed use is not public. Indeed, lawyers in such cases usually derive their fees from the compensation award—so the lawyers can be paid only if the government

succeeds in taking the property. In the overwhelming majority of eminent domain cases, the property owners have no
choice but to capitulate in the taking, and the only dispute is
over the amount of compensation. Once the lawyers receive
their share, the owners are often left with less than fair-market value.

How could such outrageous abuses exist in a free society?
The answer lies both in judicial abdication and in the voracious appetites of local governments.

Both the original constitution and the 14th Amendment
provide protections for property rights. The 14th Amendment provides that states may not deprive a person of property without due process of law. The Fifth Amendment,
which applies to the states through the 14th Amendment,
places a substantive limit on government power, providing in
relevant part that "[n]or shall private property be taken for
public use, without just compensation."

Unfortunately, the "public use" limitation was read out of
the Constitution by the U.S. Supreme Court decision in
Hawaii Housing Authority v. Midkiff.[7] In that case, fittingly
decided in 1984, the Court found that the state's use of eminent domain to combat the concentration of land ownership
and to redistribute property constituted a valid "public use."
Maybe in a socialist country, that would be true; but in a
nation grounded in the sanctity of private-property rights, it
was astonishing. What was worse was that the decision was
unanimous.

After *Midkiff,* local governments were untethered from
federal constitutional constraints to redistribute private property however they saw fit; and in all too predictable a fashion,
they proceeded to do so with reckless abandon in pursuit of
tax revenues, job creation, and grandiose redevelopment
schemes. A classic example involved the Archies, an extended

family that had spent their entire lives on land in rural Canton, Mississippi. In 2000, the state passed the "Nissan Act," which authorized the state to pour money and incentives into a new automobile plant, while authorizing the Mississippi Major Economic Impact Authority (MMEIA) to condemn properties for the new facility. The property owned by the Archies and their neighbors made up only 28 acres at the southern end of a project that would comprise 1,400 acres. Both Nissan and the former head of MMEIA admitted publicly that the project could proceed even without the Archies' land. But MMEIA pressed the fight because "[w]hat's important is the message it would send to other companies is we are unable to do what we said we would do."

Teaming up with Martin Luther King III and the Southern Christian Leadership Conference, the Institute for Justice challenged the taking in state court and secured stays against the condemnations. On the eve of consideration of the case by the Mississippi Supreme Court—and in the face of enormous public backlash—the state dismissed the eminent domain proceedings. Lonzo Archie, one of the residents whose property was saved, proclaimed, "We could not be more happy. My father and the rest of our family can now live out our days on our land."[8]

The Archies' sentiment—a fervent desire for government simply to leave them alone—is shared by many victims of eminent domain abuse around the nation. In the Cleveland suburb of Lakewood, Ohio, Jim and Joann Saleet lived in a home they called their "dream house" for 38 years, and raised four children there. The home had "all our memories in it," Joann recounted. The tidy neighborhood is perched on a cliff overlooking a park. The view is fantastic—making the neighborhood, in the eyes of the city's planners, the perfect location for a $151 million development comprising luxury homes and a shopping complex. To accomplish that goal and obtain the anticipated new tax revenues, the city deemed the neighborhood "blighted" and wielded the draconian tool of eminent domain.

"No one wants to see people lose their homes," consoled Mayor Madeline Cain, "but this is absolutely necessary for our future." Professional urban planners backed the city. If a lawsuit threatened by the Institute for Justice succeeded, warned Cleveland State University professor Edward H. Hill, "the ability of local government to recycle land will pretty much be over."[9]

Recycle land? That may be the best euphemism yet devised to depict a practice that variously has been characterized as "urban renewal," "economic redevelopment," and other beneficent-sounding terms. Usually, recycling applies to discarded products. The homes slated for bulldozing by the city of Lakewood were still a vital part of the community.

For Mayor Cain and many advocates of eminent domain, a property is ripe for taking if it can be put to "a higher and better use." In cold economic terms, that label could apply to nearly every property in America. Indeed, in Lakewood, the city deemed a home blighted if it lacked central air-conditioning or an attached two-car garage, or if its lot size was below five thousand square feet—a definition that encompassed 90 percent of the city's homes, including those owned by the mayor and every member of the city council.[10]

In human terms, there simply is no higher or better use of property than for a home. And that view ultimately (but barely) prevailed when the city's scheme was submitted to a public vote and defeated by a slender margin of 39 votes out of nearly 16,000 cast. The mayor was retired as well. Fortunately, the Saleets will be able to live out their lives in their home overlooking the park. But thousands of Americans will not be as fortunate so long as eminent domain abuse runs rampant. In a free society, the burden should be placed on the government to demonstrate that the seizure of private property is necessary to a genuine public use,* and owners should be left in a position as close as possible to the one they previously occupied.

Government does not take private property only through outright physical occupation. In many instances, it subjects property to such heavy regulation that it has the same real-world effect as a taking, usually in an effort to achieve some policy objective but to impose the costs upon one individual rather than to spread them throughout the community.[11]

The Supreme Court has always given lip service to the notion that regulation can amount to a taking, triggering an obligation of providing just compensation. But its standard historically has been nebulous—in one famous 1922 case, Justice Oliver Wendell Holmes declared, "if regulation goes too far it will be recognized as a taking"[12]—and regulations reaching the Court never seemed to go "too far."

But that began to change in the early 1990s with the case of David Lucas,[13] a South Carolina developer who bought two beachfront lots for $975,000, intending to build a house for himself on one and sell the other. The lots were in a residential area that already had been heavily developed with lovely homes.

But two years after he purchased the lots, the state enacted the Beachfront Management Act, ostensibly to address environmental concerns. Instead of purchasing Lucas's property,

*Given the dramatic expansion of government activities today—from sports facilities to water parks—in my view, "public use" for purposes of eminent domain should apply only to traditional government functions such as schools and roads. If the government is engaged in profit-making activities that compete with the private sector, it should have to resort to the free market just as other market participants must.

the state took away his right to develop it. The value of his land—which before the new law had risen to $1.2 million—was reduced by the stroke of a pen to less than zero, because Lucas would still be required to pay taxes and carry insurance on it.

The South Carolina Supreme Court agreed with the state that Lucas should bear the burden of the diminution of the value of his property because the law advanced a public interest. But in a landmark ruling, the U.S. Supreme Court held that the law was in effect a taking of Lucas's property, because it deprived the owner of all of the property's value and was not necessary to abate a nuisance.[14]

Ironically, once the state was forced to compensate Lucas to obtain his land, it decided that its environmental concerns weren't worth the money, and sold the lots to another developer. It is enlightening to observe how rationally government can act when it has to bear the costs of its own regulations.

Though the *Lucas* decision was an important step forward for the rights of property owners, the Court's present takings jurisprudence still contains huge loopholes that allow government to run roughshod over property rights without paying just compensation. One loophole is the Court's rule that in order to trigger compensation, a regulation must deprive the owner of 100 percent of the value of the property at issue. As a result, enterprising local governments now often make sure to leave the owner at least a modicum of the property value—say, 5 percent—in order to avoid a finding that the property was taken. That means that oppressive laws such as historical-preservation ordinances, which deprive owners of the ability to alter or renovate their homes, or rent-control ordinances, which often limit property owners' ability to collect a fair return on investment or to control who lives in the property, are extremely difficult to challenge, at least under the takings clause.

Another loophole is the rule stating that in order for a regulatory taking to be "ripe" for judicial challenge, there must be a final government decision. That requires first an actual decision by government, then the exhaustion of all manner of administrative appeals. In the best of circumstances, this process can take years. But clever governments often frustrate any realistic chance of legal challenge by declining ever to reach a final decision—which of course serves the goals of slow-growth advocates by preventing development even though theoretically the process is proceeding.[15]

Those skewed rules leave property owners vulnerable to government extortion—sure, we'll grant your development permit, if you agree "voluntarily" to build us a park—and unfortunately, too many governments engage in precisely such practices. In 1994, the Supreme Court recognized this practice, and set out to put an end to it. Florence Dolan, an elderly widow, wanted to expand her hardware store in Tigard, Oregon. Fine, said the city, as long as you build us a new bicycle path and dedicate an area of your property as a public greenway. The Court ruled in a 5-4 decision that in order to expropriate part of Mrs. Dolan's property without just compensation as a condition to receiving a variance, the government would have to show both that an "essential nexus" existed between the costs imposed upon the community by proposed development and the conditions sought by the city, and that there was a "rough proportionality" between the development burden and the conditions.[16] In this case, the expansion of the store likely would increase vehicular traffic, so that the city reasonably could have required Mrs. Dolan to reimburse it for added street lanes or traffic signals. But the requirement of building a bicycle path or dedicating

a greenway bore little relationship to the costs imposed upon
the city by the store expansion. They were very simply goodies
the city desired. So the Court overturned the lower court's
decision sustaining the confiscatory exactions.

The *Dolan* decision especially could aid individual property owners burdened by excessive government demands in
return for permission to develop property. But in the real
world, developers often merely cave in to such demands,
because they must deal with the city over and over again.
Property owners who fight back may find that the city has
many other tools available to make their lives miserable. That
is the heart of the conundrum: We cannot protect our property rights unless we are willing to stand up for them; but
many property owners conclude that it is easier and less costly
to capitulate than to fight. That tendency pushes the pendu-
lum away from the sanctity of property rights toward an ever-
encroaching erosion of liberty. Decisions such as *Lucas* and
Dolan demonstrate that for those who are willing to fight
back, justice can triumph.

Yet another systemic abuse of property rights is civil asset
forfeiture. It's a story of cops and robbers—except in this
instance, they're sometimes one and the same.

Young Jesse Robles learned that painful lesson one evening in 2003 when he was visiting friends. A knock on the
door turned out to be two police officers, who announced that
it smelled like "Cheech and Chong" and proceeded to enter
the house and search it. They found no evidence of drug use.
Eventually, they opened a safe, and inside was $1,600 and a
marijuana cigarette. The money belonged to Robles, who
kept his earnings from his pizza job in his friend's safe. No
one was charged with any wrongdoing, but the cops kept the
money, which went into the police coffers. It sounds more
like something that would happen in an authoritarian coun-

try: no warrant, no charges, no arrest; but the police keep the cash. How could such a scenario occur—with frequency—in a free society?

Pursuant to the practice of civil asset forfeiture, when the police suspect that certain property is connected to a crime, the government may seize it, under the "legal fiction" that the property itself is guilty of the crime. Indeed, the property rather than the owner is the named defendant in the case.*

Starting from that rather bizarre premise, the applicable rules are, perhaps not surprisingly, rather skewed against the individual. That is because whereas an individual charged with a crime is afforded extensive constitutional protections, asset forfeiture is subject to civil rather than criminal rules. In other words, there is no presumption of innocence. The government need only demonstrate, by a preponderance of the evidence, that the property was in some way connected to an unlawful activity.[17] No charges need have been filed against anyone for commission of the underlying crime. Most distressingly, no "innocent owner" defense exists: the owner whose property is forfeited need have no connection with illegal activity. If a home is rented to someone who engages in prostitution, it can be seized even though the landlord has no knowledge of it; if a mortgaged home is used for drug possession, it can be seized with the mortgage company bearing the loss.†

---

*That phenomenon leads to odd case captions, such as the one in the New Jersey case discussed below, *State of New Jersey v. One 1990 Ford Thunderbird*.

†Fighting asset forfeiture laws can make for strange bedfellows, with mortgage companies teaming up with criminal-defense attorneys to fight government overreaching. IJ filed an *amicus curiae* brief in one case, *U.S. v. James Daniel Good Real Property*, 510 U.S. 43 (1993), in which the U.S. Supreme Court ruled that the government must provide notice before seizing certain types of assets. Afterward, Mr. Good wrote IJ a letter expressing his gratitude for defending his property rights, and noting that while the

That's what Tina Bennis found out after her husband was arrested for soliciting a prostitute. As a double whammy for the unfortunate Mrs. Bennis, he was using her car at the time. The police seized the car, and she tried to recover it, arguing that she had nothing to do with the crime. But while acknowledging that obvious fact, the U.S. Supreme Court held that her innocence was irrelevant: The *car* had been involved in the crime; therefore, it could be confiscated.[18]

Making civil asset forfeiture even more subject to abuse is the widespread practice of the federal government and many states of allowing law-enforcement officials to retain the seized assets for their own use and benefit. That practice creates a strong financial incentive for such officials to wield asset forfeiture as frequently and broadly as possible—and violates the due-process right of individuals to have impartial officials making objective decisions at every turn. Not surprisingly, the combination of the war on drugs and the desire of law-enforcement officials to sweeten their coffers has contributed to escalating use of the civil-asset-forfeiture power.

In 1999, the 17-year-old son of Cumberland County, New Jersey, deputy sheriff Carol Thomas was arrested for dealing drugs. Unfortunately for Ms. Thomas, at the time of her son's arrest, he was driving her 1990 Ford Thunderbird. The police seized the car, which was owned and paid for by Carol Thomas. To put it mildly, she was completely unaware that her son was dealing drugs, for which he was duly prosecuted.

Because she had no defense as an innocent owner, Thomas counterclaimed against the state, challenging the state policy allowing police to retain seized assets. Repre-

---

case was argued he was in Central America fighting for the Sandinistas. Most IJ supporters and beneficiaries exhibit a somewhat more consistent support for private-property rights.

sented by the Institute for Justice, Ms. Thomas obtained evidence that over the course of three years, state law-enforcement authorities had collected $32 million in asset forfeitures. They used the proceeds for all manner of goodies. The Gloucester County prosecutor spent $733.96 on bagels and $21,000 on travel and hotels. The Morris County prosecutor (who is now a judge) used $29,000 of seized assets for a "chiefs retreat" at the Seaview Marriott Resort, a posh golf course and resort on the Jersey Shore. He also purchased exercise equipment. The Essex County prosecutor spent nearly $5,000 for an executive retreat at the Pleasantville Chateau, a luxurious faux-castle in West Orange. He also spent nearly $30,000 on interior decorating (perhaps making his the only prosecutor's office in the nation to be professionally decorated). The Warren County prosecutor spent $340 on a golf game.[19]

State trial court judge G. Thomas Bowen struck down the statute as a violation of due process, ruling that "the augmentation of the county prosecutors' budgets . . . provides to those in prosecutorial functions financial interests which are not so remote as to escape the taint of impermissible bias in enforcement of the laws."[20] Although the ruling was made under both the federal and state constitutions, it had no immediate effect beyond the boundaries of the Garden State, meaning that additional lawsuits will be necessary to curb such abusive practices in other states.

Government violates private-property rights in ways other than regulating or taking property. Several cities have enacted inspection laws, especially aimed at rental properties, that allow city officials to enter and search the premises without a warrant, notice, or consent of the owners, ostensibly to check for violations of various city codes. Such a law in the Chicago suburb of Park Forest, Illinois, also charged a $60 fee for tenants who refused to allow their homes to be searched and who forced police officers to obtain a warrant. Richard Reinbold, a landlord, challenged the law on behalf of his tenants in a suit filed by the Institute for Justice. "In my opinion, this is the housing Gestapo," Reinbold proclaimed. "We don't want to live in a Fourth Amendment–free zone."[21] Federal district judge Joan Gottschall struck down the law in part,[22] and the city subsequently repealed it. But like a bad penny, similar rental-housing inspection laws continue to crop up around the country.

A number of themes emerge from these examples of grassroots tyranny taking the form of violations of private-property rights. First, like economic liberty, private-property rights are a freedom that most Americans think they have, until the government takes them away. Second, while many people equate property with wealth, the preservation of private-property rights is of vital and intimate concern to every American. It is still a cornerstone of the American Dream to own a home and to secure the comforts of modern life. That dream often is rendered illusory when government can regulate or take property on the barest of pretenses. Indeed, it is those at the bottom of the economic ladder who least possess the knowledge and resources to take on city hall.

Moreover, just as with our other rights, we all have a vested stake in protecting private-property rights, even if we may be able to gain a momentary advantage in their violation. The powerful developer who today invokes a city's power of eminent domain to secure desired property may tomorrow suffer the same fate if the city decides that property could be put to better use or should be subject to confiscatory development restrictions.

During the New Deal, the U.S. Supreme Court relegated property and economic rights to second-class status, inferior to "fundamental" rights such as freedom of speech.[23] Since that time, both property rights and economic liberty have received little protection, despite their central importance to our nation's doctrinal devotion to individual liberty and the free-enterprise system.

Over the last few years, private-property rights have experienced something of a renaissance. In the *Dolan* case, Chief Justice William Rehnquist remarked, "we see no reason why the Takings Clause, as much a part of the Bill of Rights as the First Amendment or Fourth Amendment, should be relegated to the status of a poor relation."[24] At an even more fundamental level, Justice Anthony Kennedy has declared it an "essential principle" that "[i]ndividual freedom finds tangible expression in property rights."[25]

We should hope that a majority of the justices retain those insights and act upon them. With vigilance and a willingness to fight to protect our precious liberties, perhaps such insights will not only once again permeate American jurisprudence, but will also inform the decisions of government officials so that they will act with appropriate self-restraint in exercising powers that touch upon these important rights.

6

Freedom
of Speech

A federal judge has ruled that the City of New Orleans
cannot ban sidewalk book sales because it violates the
First Amendment. Here's what I don't understand. Why
did New Orleans decide to ban book sales? You ever been
to New Orleans? People are drinking on the sidewalk.
They're taking their tops off on the sidewalks. They're
urinating on the sidewalks. They just don't want people
reading on the sidewalk.

—Jay Leno, *The Tonight Show*,
NBC (June 19, 2003)

FOR A LONG time, Josh Wexler and Anne Jordan Blanton
wanted to open a sidewalk book stand on the streets of New
Orleans, a first step toward their dream of one day owning
their own bookstore. When they went to the city to obtain a
permit, they learned that they could secure permission to sell
such items as razor blades, pencils, and shoelaces—but not
books. In fact, the bureaucrats wouldn't even give them an
application. "We're not attempting to cause any trouble or get
anything special from the government," Blanton explained.
"We just want to earn an honest living sharing our love of
books."

City officials too often seem to derive malicious pleasure

in denying people the chance to realize their dreams, and it seemed about to happen this time as well. But fortunately Wexler and Blanton had a tool at their disposal that is usually unavailable to secure entrepreneurial freedoms: the First Amendment. The first command of the Bill of Rights — "Congress shall make no law abridging freedom of speech" — applies through the 14th Amendment to state and local governments. As applied by conservative and liberal courts alike, the free-speech clause has proved a powerful weapon against governments' constant efforts to repress speech.

So too did it secure the rights of the young entrepreneurs in New Orleans.[1] Represented by the Institute for Justice, Wexler and Blanton secured a permanent injunction against the city. The city is "charged with the obligation of drafting ordinances that avoid trampling on First Amendment freedoms," declared federal district court Judge Stanwood R. Duval.[2] The city had defended the law as a reasonable regulation of the time, place, and manner of speech. The judge rejected that defense. "An ordinance, like the one the City of New Orleans adopted, that operates as a blanket ban on book selling or under the City's interpretation, prohibits book selling from a small easily moveable table is an unreasonable restriction that does not provide ample, alternative means of communication."

Still, despite their generally good record in enforcing an unequivocal constitutional command,[3] the courts have created a hierarchy of First Amendment values that receive varying degrees of protection. At the top of the hierarchy is political speech, of which government regulations (notwithstanding the Supreme Court's disappointing decisions regarding restrictions of campaign contributions) trigger the strictest scrutiny. In many areas, the courts generally have protected even offensive speech, such as flag-burning and the right to view pornography. But at the bottom of the hierarchy is commercial speech—that is, speech intended to propose a commercial transaction. Suppression or regulation of commercial speech invokes much lower judicial scrutiny than other types of speech.

That juxtaposition—greater judicial protection for pornography than for commercial speech—is startling. The First Amendment uses the term "speech," with no differentiation among its types. Indeed, the courts in other contexts have taken a broad view of the concept, protecting even such "symbolic" speech as cross-burning. Moreover, the United States is emphatically a commercial republic. In today's society, commercial information (such as drug prices), whether conveyed in traditional media or over the Internet, is arguably as important—if not more so to many people—as political speech. To return to a theme from the first chapter, ask a person on the street who his or her mayor is, and you'll probably evoke a blank stare; ask for the names of long-distance telephone providers and you'll probably get a half-dozen. Surely most Americans spend much more time reading about commercial products than politics, indicating their subjective priorities. In my own household, "Don't throw out the advertisements" is a common command; indeed, my wife even subscribes to a popular magazine *about shopping*, a subject upon which a majority of the subscribers likely are already quite expert.

But the importance most people attach to commercial speech is not always reflected in local government policy. Edward Salib owns a Winchell's Donuts on the corner of Main Street and Country Club Drive in Mesa, Arizona (yes— the very same corner from which the city tried to erase Randy Bailey's brake shop). Over the course of several months, his store was the subject of intense law-enforcement scrutiny by the city, which dispatched one of its 27 "code enforcers" repeatedly to monitor the store, eventually filling an 80-page file.

His suspected crime? Selling drugs? Harboring criminal activity?

No, hanging signs.

Like millions of business owners, Salib relies on signs to attract customers into his business. Periodically, Salib receives standardized signs from the company, advertising donut specials, cappuccino, and the like, which he hangs in his windows.

Or he did, until the city told Salib that he was violating its sign ordinance, which forbade signs occupying more than 30 percent of a window space. The rule was hopelessly arbitrary and irrational, with its percentage based on an average derived from other cities' ordinances. If a store had bigger windows, it could have bigger signs. There was not much Salib could do about the size of the company's standard signs, so he asked if he could leave one window empty, resulting in an average of 30 percent of the total windows being covered. No dice, the city replied: The restriction applies to each window. Because Salib had no control over the size of the advertisements, the effect of the ordinance would be to prevent him from advertising altogether.

The ordinance was motivated by city officials' anger over another store whose windows were completely covered over with paint. But ironically, that store was exempted from the law by a grandfather clause. Salib's signs were grandfathered, too, until he took down the ads and put up new ones.

The city grasped for post hoc justifications for the ordinance. One explanation was that part of the windows had to remain clear so the police could look in. But in the case of a donut shop, that isn't necessary because in many instances the police often are already munching donuts inside. The

Institute for Justice Arizona Chapter once again took Mesa to court—to date, the only city it has sued twice—challenging the sign ordinance as a violation under both the federal and state constitutions.[4] A trial court upheld the ordinance—illustrating the low regard for commercial speech under current law—and the case is now on appeal.

While Edward Salib was battling local bureaucrats in a desert suburb, Dennis Ballen was facing a similar ordeal in the Pacific Northwest. Several years ago, Ballen lost his job. Instead of finding another one, he started his own business, Blazing Bagels, in Redmond, Washington. I can personally attest to the quality of Ballen's bagels. Trouble is, the shop is located in a strip of warehouses off a main street. Given the paucity of pedestrian traffic, Ballen needed to lure customers off the main drag.

So he hired Daniel Pickard to stand on the main street wearing a sandwich board bearing the words, "Fresh Bagels Now Open." Taking on the job with gusto, Pickard danced and used the sign as an air guitar, attracting smiles from passing motorists and, more importantly, business for Blazing Bagels.

But the human advertising campaign didn't last long. The City of Redmond wielded its sign ordinance, threatening Ballen with fines up to $5,000. "Now my sign guy's afraid to go out there, that they'll arrest him," Ballen said. "He's so afraid he won't even carry a protest sign."

After the city yanked Pickard off the street, Blazing Bagels saw its sales plummet 35 percent, and Ballen faced the prospect of losing his business altogether. The city justifies its ordinance as a means of preventing traffic distractions and preserving aesthetics. But at the same time that it prohibits most commercial signs, the city allows signs for other activities, such as announcing events, promoting political campaigns, and selling or leasing real estate. So that were Ballen to display a sign that read "For Sale: Blazing Bagels," the legality of the sign would depend on whether Ballen was selling his store or his bagels.

The Institute for Justice Washington Chapter filed a lawsuit challenging the sign ordinance under the free-speech protections of the federal and state constitutions.[5] In January 2004, the federal district court in Seattle issued a preliminary injunction against the ordinance, finding the city's discriminatory policy troublesome. "There is no evidence in the record that the banned signs are less aesthetically appealing or more harmful to pedestrian traffic than the permitted signs," the court declared. "The City must do more than argue the importance of deferring to the legislative judgment to succeed . . . ; the City has the burden of showing that the Ordinance's ten categories of exempted signs do not undermine and counteract the asserted interests of the City."[6] Though the injunction means that Ballen can advertise his business while the case continues, the opinion underscores the reality that under current jurisprudence, the city potentially could ban *all* commercial signs so long as it did so in a nondiscriminatory way.

Those two cases are part of an ongoing effort to increase judicial scrutiny for commercial speech by eliminating the jurisprudential dichotomy between commercial and other types of speech—or at least to boost state constitutional protection of commercial speech beyond the current federal constitutional standards. A victory would not necessarily mean a proliferation of tacky signs—local governments still could reasonably regulate the time, place, or manner of speech. But it would force local governments to calibrate their restrictions carefully, recognizing the vital importance of commercial speech to businesses and consumers alike.

Sometimes the line between political and commercial speech is blurry, which exacerbates the problems created by the courts' multiple tiers of scrutiny in the speech context. If the speech is categorized as commercial speech, the right to political speech can be the proverbial baby that is thrown out with the bathwater.

Beginning in 1996, a group of activists began publicizing allegations that Nike and its subcontractors were engaged in unfair and illegal labor practices in foreign countries, violating minimum-wage and maximum-hours laws, subjecting laborers to abuse, and unlawfully exposing them to harsh chemicals and other unsafe working conditions. Reports of those allegations appeared on *48 Hours* and in a host of national publications.

Nike struck back, denying the charges and projecting a positive image of its labor practices, in the form of news releases, correspondence, and full-page newspaper advertisements. Among other things, the company publicized a report by former United Nations ambassador Andrew Young, which found no evidence of illegal or unsafe working conditions in Nike factories.

Regardless of which side had it right—or if both sides had a bit of the truth—the debate exemplified precisely the no-holds-barred give and take on issues of vital public concern that the First Amendment was designed to protect. In public debate, the First Amendment protects even untruthful statements—witness almost any speech by every politician—subject to rules of libel and slander. Likewise, in debate over issues of public concern, the government is not ever supposed to take sides, tipping the balance to one side or the other. Rather, both sides are at liberty to use whatever mechanisms are at their disposal to make their views known.

Unfortunately, the state of California abandoned its constitutionally ordained neutrality. The anti-Nike activists invoked the state's consumer-protection laws to file a false-advertising claim against Nike, seeking to force Nike to disgorge any profits tied to its advertisements and to engage in a court-approved "public information" campaign.

The California courts should have ruled in favor of Nike. A rule exposing companies to liability for defending themselves against charges of wrongdoing would have an enormously chilling effect on speech about issues of enormous public importance. As companies such as Microsoft, ExxonMobil, and Pfizer attested in a brief supporting Nike, exposing businesses to long and costly litigation over statements about public-policy issues or business practices would force them to stay silent in the face of public criticism.[7]

Moreover, it would unbalance the level First Amendment playing field by allowing critics to raise reckless and untrue charges while forcing the object of the critics to meet a meticulous standard of accuracy, with truth in the eye of the judicial beholder. Given that many such debates are far from black and white, it would create great risk to those accused of wrongdoing who dare to stand up for themselves.

The trial and appellate courts obeyed the clear command of the First Amendment, dismissing the claims against Nike. But the California Supreme Court, by a 4-3 margin, reversed and reinstated the case. The majority noted that false statements in a commercial speech context are not accorded First Amendment protection. Even though Nike's advertisements did not fit the classic definition of commercial speech—that is, speech that proposes a commercial transaction—the Court found that Nike's motivation was economic, and that the debate might affect consumers' decisions about whether to buy Nike's products. Therefore, if Nike's assertions were found to be false, the company could be held liable for false advertising.[8]

Justice Janice Brown, a vigilant defender of individual liberties, launched her dissent with an attack on current First Amendment jurisprudence. "In 1942, the United States Supreme Court, like a wizard trained at Hogwarts, waved its wand and 'plucked the commercial speech doctrine out of thin air'."[9] Under the doctrine, she charged, all speech is *either* commercial or noncommercial, and commercial speech "receives less protection than noncommercial speech."[10] She urged a more nuanced approach that takes into account the different types of speech encompassed within the broad definition of commercial speech, and concluded that treating all forms of commercial speech the same way would have a deleterious impact on the free flow of ideas. "Making Nike strictly liable for any false or misleading representations about its labor practices stifles Nike's ability to participate in a public debate *initiated by others*."[11]

The United States Supreme Court granted review, but ultimately decided to remand the case to the lower courts for further deliberations without reaching the merits.[12] Thereafter, Nike settled with the plaintiffs, paying them $1.5 million to make the lawsuit go away, thereby establishing a precedent that indicates lawsuits of this type may be lucrative for anti-corporation activists, and emboldening such activists to go after other companies.

The California Supreme Court majority's broad definition of commercial speech and its flimsy protection for discussion of public issues in that context could have broad ramifications for the free speech of companies and those who work for them. Corporations often have an eye out for the bottom line whenever they "speak" in public, but that doesn't render their speech on public-policy issues any less important or sacrosanct than anyone else's, and certainly doesn't justify protecting it less. After the *Kasky* decision, what if a company speaks out on a widely debated policy issue—like free trade or taxes—and makes a statement found to be false? What if a corporation sponsors a play in which characters do so? Are unions and other players in the marketplace subject to similar constraints? At the very least, the decision will make companies and others similarly bound think twice before engaging in controversial speech—and it relegates them to the status of second-class entities with regard to the First Amendment.

Which is exactly what businesses in Las Cruces, New Mexico, recently discovered. The city prohibits political signs on commercial property except for campaign-related signs posted within 90 days of an election. Other political signs, announcing support for abortion rights or opposition to gun control, require a permit from the city. Prior to the February 3, 2004, presidential caucus, several businesses posted signs supporting Democratic candidates: Howard Dean or Wesley Clark. But the city ordered them to take the signs down. Why? Because a caucus is "a selection and not an election," explained Deputy City Attorney Harry "Pete" Connelly, so the signs are not allowed. "It would be simple to just amend the ordinance to include a caucus," Connelly added, "but we haven't gotten there yet."[13] Until the bureaucrats get around to changing the law, apparently, political speech will be suppressed.

Contemporary local government violations of free speech extend beyond merely restricting commercial and political speech. As dangerous and offensive to the First Amendment as suppression of speech is, equally repugnant is compelled speech, where people are forced to support ideas with which they disagree. Yet that phenomenon is taking place with increasing frequency as states move toward subsidizing candidates in political campaigns. The most sweeping effort is Arizona's so-called Clean Elections Act, which was narrowly approved in a voter initiative. The law showers massive subsidies on participating candidates who collect the requisite

number of $5 contributions, even as it seriously limits contri-
butions to those who prefer to run for office without taxpayer
subsidies. The result is to skew the election system in favor of
subsidized candidates and against those running solely with
voluntary contributions.[14]

Funding for the program was earmarked from three
sources: a 10 percent surcharge on all civil and criminal fines,
which accounted for most of the funding; a $100 annual fee
collected from lobbyists for for-profit entities; and state
income tax deductions and credits. Few Arizonans realize that
if they incur a parking fine or a speeding ticket, they will also
be involuntarily contributing to candidates not of their choosing.

It is a hallmark of a free society that participation in politics must be voluntary. Typically, only in authoritarian nations
does turnout in elections approach 100 percent—remarkably,
often all for the same unopposed candidate. American courts
universally have held that campaign contributions are a form
of political speech; and that individuals cannot be forced to
support beliefs with which they disagree, such as participating in the flag salute. By enacting the Clean Elections Act,
Arizona joined the dark side, transforming a deeply intimate
personal choice—whether or not to contribute to a political
candidate—from a voluntary one into an object of government coercion.

The Institute for Justice challenged the involuntary funding sources as a violation of the federal and state constitutions. One plaintiff, Steve May, incurred a parking ticket, to
which was added a surcharge for campaign subsidies. Adding
insult to injury, May was a state legislator who was running
without public subsidies against candidates who were receiving them. That meant May was being forced to contribute to
his opponents' campaigns. Joining May as a plaintiff was Rick

Lavis, a lobbyist for Arizona cotton growers, who objected to subsidizing candidates with which his organization disagreed.

The trial court struck down the lobbyist fee, but upheld the surcharge.[15] The court of appeals struck down the surcharge, concluding that it was impermissible compelled speech, but this decision was overturned by the Arizona Supreme Court.[16] The U.S. Supreme Court declined to review the decision.

Fortunately, the beast may yet be slayed. In January 2004, the Institute for Justice Arizona Chapter filed a new challenge, this time in federal court. The plaintiffs are an advocacy group that objects to the subsidies given to match independent expenditures and thereby diluting the group's message; as well as past and future candidates who object to the rules of the game that reward candidates who participate in the subsidy system while punishing those who do not. A new initiative forbidding subsidies to politicians is slated for the November 2004 ballot. In a time of soaring state budget deficits, it is difficult to imagine that voters will assign a high priority to bankrolling political campaigns with taxpayer money. A nonbinding referendum to repeal campaign subsidies in Massachusetts in 2002 was supported by three-quarters of the state's electorate. If the residents of one of the nation's most liberal states resoundingly opposed subsidies for politicians, perhaps the zeal for this particular type of "reform" will die a well-deserved death.

Given that freedom of speech is perhaps our most vibrant liberty, it is remarkable how many attempts persist to suppress speech—ranging from controversial art exhibits to "offensive speech" on college campuses—or to compel it. Free speech is vital to democracy and a free society. Let's hope that the courts will be even more aggressive in protecting that vital liberty—and that governments will grow a bit more restrained in abridging it.

7

The Right to Be Left Alone

AT A 2003 legislative hearing on a bill to limit eminent domain abuse, Arizona State Senator Ken Cheuvront quipped that he wished that his colleagues who cared so much about the sanctity of private-property rights would extend such protections to the bedroom. He was exactly right. Too few policymakers who believe that government's power to take or regulate private property must be kept in check apply the same logic to protecting certain consensual activities inside the home. Unfortunately, on the flip side, too few policymakers who believe in the sanctity of the bedroom seem to extend the sanctuary to protection of the home itself.* That is why we have the Constitution and the Bill of Rights: to establish a higher authority, a rule of law, to objectify the boundaries of permissible government interference with personal autonomy.[1]

Individualism is both an American persona and an American ideal. Our nation was founded by people escaping religious persecution and seeking opportunity. Because of the belief that people should when possible stand on their own feet, our social welfare system is much smaller than that of other modern societies. As a collective matter, we generally want from our government only what we cannot provide to ourselves (though just as James Madison predicted, special-interest groups constantly seek special benefits for themselves). Conversely, the thing most of us want from government—when we don't need it for some particular purpose— is to leave us alone.

That, of course, is more easily desired than achieved. Whether on the basis of competing moral beliefs or a mere desire to control other people's lives, government is constantly meddling in the intimate affairs of people's lives, often legislating to the lowest common denominator and restricting liberty in the process.

Often those intrusions conflict with vital constitutional traditions, such as freedom of association and the right to privacy. Neither of those rights expressly appears in the Constitution; and yet most Americans treasure them even as they often take them for granted. Government often defends its restrictions by noting that those freedoms do not appear in the constitutional text, and therefore are not judicially enforceable. Yet they flow logically from a confluence of

*True to liberal form, Cheuvront voted against the bill.

expressly stated rights, such as freedom of speech, private-property rights, due process, equal protection, and in some instances freedom of religion. Moreover, the argument that privacy and freedom of association do not exist requires reading the Ninth and Fourteenth Amendments—and their protection of unenumerated rights and the privileges or immunities of citizens—out of the Constitution;[2] and viewing the Constitution as a charter of rights rather than as a restriction on the power of government. Plainly, our system of government, grounded in common law and the principle of individual sovereignty, creates a zone of personal autonomy into which the government may not permissibly intrude except with compelling justification. A proper view of the Constitution provides substantial protection for the right to be left alone.

Yet another reason why this generic right has eroded is that, once again, too few Americans are willing to honor it if they are offended by the way that other people exercise it. If a right is respected not absolutely, but depending only upon whose ox is being gored, it will fade away.

All of these themes are illustrated by a pair of recent Supreme Court rulings that protected the right to be left alone. Both involved people engaged in private, consensual activities into which the government intervened because the activity offended the moral beliefs of a political majority. Both touched upon the community's attitudes toward homosexuality. In both cases, the Court vindicated the liberty of the individuals involved to control their own destinies. The decisions invoked essentially the same principles. Yet, ironically, very few people—including the justices themselves—agreed with both decisions.[3] Instead, most of the justices as well as most Americans agreed with one outcome but not the other, indulging their own moral preferences rather than supporting consistently the right to be left alone that most Americans cherish. As with all rights, the right to be left alone cannot endure if we honor it only when it suits our personal predilections. It is in this climate of constitutional relativism that grassroots tyranny flourishes.

The more recent of the two cases was decided in 2003. It started when police in Houston, Texas, responded to a complaint about a disturbance involving weapons. When they arrived at the private residence in question, inside they found two occupants, John Lawrence and Tyron Garner, engaged in a consensual sexual act. The police arrested the two men and charged them with the crime of engaging in "deviate sexual intercourse with another individual of the same sex." The Texas statute defines deviate sexual intercourse as homosexual sodomy or oral sex.[4]

Seventeen years earlier, in a similar case entitled *Bowers v. Hardwick*, the Court by a 5-4 majority upheld a similar Georgia anti-sodomy statute, finding that the Constitution does not confer "a fundamental right upon homosexuals to engage in sodomy."[5] Of course it doesn't. Nor does it expressly state a right to privacy, freedom of association, freedom of enterprise, or other important vital restraints on the power of government. All of those rights were intended to be protected by broadly worded constitutional provisions that protect a wide range of individual liberties. But that is beside the point. Rather, the relevant constitutional inquiry should entail whether government *possesses the power* to forbid or restrict the conduct at issue. And it was in that fashion that the Court revisited *Bowers* and confronted the case of Lawrence and Garner.

By a 6-3 vote, the Court struck down the discriminatory

Texas anti-sodomy law,* with five justices voting to overturn *Bowers v. Hardwick*. Writing for the majority, Justice Anthony Kennedy framed the case in these terms: "Liberty protects the person from unwarranted government intrusions into a dwelling or other private places. In our tradition the State is not omnipresent in the home."[6] By placing the case in terms of broad liberty and by invoking private-property rights, Kennedy took the issue out of the realm of a narrow "right" to homosexual sodomy and placed it within a more universal framework of freedom from governmental intrusion that pervades our Constitution.

Noting that the Court had protected liberties such as the right of privacy and the right of parents to direct the upbringing of their children under the liberty provision of the 14th Amendment's due process clause, Kennedy determined this issue should be decided under the same analysis. While the anti-sodomy statutes only purported to forbid certain sexual practices, he observed, "[t]heir penalties and purposes, though, have more far-reaching consequences, touching upon the most private human conduct, sexual behavior, and in the most private of places, the home."[7] Acknowledging that "for centuries there have been powerful voices to condemn homosexual conduct as immoral," the Court nonetheless recognized that "[t]he issue is whether the majority may use the power of the State to enforce these views on the whole society through operation of the criminal law."[8]

Given that the conduct was private, intimate, and not harmful, the Court concluded the answer was no. The Court cited a proposition from an earlier case that set down a bed-

---

*The law was discriminatory because it prohibited homosexual sodomy but allowed heterosexual sodomy. The Georgia law upheld in *Bowers*, by contrast, outlawed all sodomy.

rock principle of a free society: "It is a promise of the Constitution that there is a realm of personal liberty which the government may not enter."[9] Applying that principle, the Court concluded, "[this] case does involve two adults who, with full and mutual consent from each other, engaged in sexual practices common to a homosexual lifestyle. The petitioners are entitled to respect for their private lives."*

In dissent, Justice Antonin Scalia saw nothing transcendent about the principles involved in the case. "Today's opinion is the product of a Court, which is the product of a law-profession culture, that has largely signed on to the so-called homosexual agenda," he declared, "by which I mean the agenda promoted by some homosexual activists directed at eliminating the moral opprobrium that has traditionally attached to homosexual conduct."[10] He noted that "[m]any Americans do not want persons who openly engage in homosexual conduct as partners in their business, as scoutmasters for their children, as teachers in their children's schools, or as boarders in their home."[11]

But the decision does not force individuals to interact in their daily social or business lives with homosexuals. Indeed, it should stand for exactly the opposite premise: that just as homosexuals should be free to engage in intimate social contact, particularly in the privacy of their own homes, so too should people be free not to interact. Moreover, conservative justices like Scalia ordinarily would never countenance police intrusion into the home absent harmful activity. Why would they deny the same sanctuary to individuals just because they happen to be gay?

---

*Justice Kennedy was joined in his opinion by Justices John Paul Stevens, David Souter, Ruth Bader Ginsburg, and Stephen Breyer. Justice Sandra Day O'Connor concurred in the result, but would have decided the case on equal-protection grounds and would not have overruled *Bowers*.

Ultimately, Scalia resorted to majoritarianism, declaring "it is the premise of our system that those judgments are going to be made by the people, and not imposed by a governing caste that knows best."[12] Likewise, though Justice Clarence Thomas found the law "'uncommonly silly'," he voted to uphold it because he could find neither a right to privacy nor a right to liberty of the person in the Constitution.[13]

Yet when those same conservative justices saw the tables turned—that is when democratic processes acted to *protect* homosexuals—they found that a right that does not expressly appear in the Constitution—the right to expressive association—*should* override that majoritarian preference. At the same time, four of the liberal justices retreated behind the rubric of federalism to repudiate the very freedom of association they found so important in *Lawrence*.

That earlier case involved that most nostalgic of all American institutions, the Boy Scouts. The Scouts seek to instill a certain set of moral values, based upon a belief in God. Whether right or wrong, they deeply believe that homosexuality is incompatible with their mission.

But the state of New Jersey believed otherwise. The case involved James Dale, a former Eagle Scout who as an adult served as an assistant scoutmaster. When the Scouts learned that Dale was an avowed homosexual and a gay-rights activist, they decided he was not a proper role model for the boys and revoked his adult membership. But the state invoked its civil-rights law, which forbade discrimination on the basis of sexual orientation in public accommodations. Finding that the Scouts fit the definition of "public accommodation," the New Jersey courts ruled that they would have to reinstate Dale.

Whether or not one finds discrimination against homosexuals appealing or abhorrent, it seems difficult to rationalize denying individuals or social groups the autonomy to decide whether to privately socialize with people whose lifestyles they deem morally—sometimes even religiously—offensive. Imagine the reaction of the New Jersey courts if a gay fraternity were forced under notions of nondiscrimination to admit gay-bashers into their midst; or a black sorority to admit avowed members of the Ku Klux Klan. All such government compulsion should offend the sensibilities of anyone who believes in freedom of association. And indeed, even though freedom of association is not written into the Constitution, exceptions to the principle have traditionally been tolerated only for the most compelling of reasons—such as to remedy past government-sanctioned discrimination in the Civil Rights Act of 1964.

Yet the Supreme Court divided 5-4 in reversing the decision of the New Jersey courts under the federal constitution and upholding the Boy Scouts' freedom of association. Chief Justice William Rehnquist and Justices Scalia and Thomas, who would later vote to deny freedom of intimate association in *Lawrence*, voted for the Boy Scouts in the *Dale* case; while Justices Stevens, Souter, Ginsburg, and Breyer pulled the opposite flip-flop. Only Justices O'Connor and Kennedy sided with freedom of association in both cases. The justices' situational constitutionalism reflected the positions of advocacy groups who submitted briefs. Few supported both the right of homosexuals to associate freely and the freedom of the Boy Scouts not to associate with them.* Fortunately, the

---

*The Institute for Justice, representing Gays and Lesbians for Individual Liberty (GLIL), submitted briefs on the winning side in both cases. In *Dale*, GLIL and the Boy Scouts made interesting bedfellows, so to speak. However repugnant the Boy Scouts' stance toward homosexuals, GLIL reasoned that if there is one group in America that needs to stand up for freedom of association more than any other, it is homosexuals. Their fidelity to principle was vindicated three years later in *Lawrence*.

swing justices led the Court as a whole to uphold the principle in both cases.

Ironically, the right asserted by the Boy Scouts in their brief could have been taken word for word by the gay couple in *Lawrence*: the right, under the federal constitution, "to enter into and maintain . . . intimate or private relationships."[14] The New Jersey courts had rejected that claim, finding that the Boy Scouts were not "'sufficiently personal or private to warrant constitutional protection' under the freedom of intimate association."[15]

But the Court, in a decision by Chief Justice Rehnquist, disagreed. "'[I]mplicit in the right to engage in activities protected by the First Amendment'," he declared, "is 'a corresponding right to associate with others in pursuit of a wide variety of political, social, economic, educational, religious and cultural ends'." Moreover, "'freedom of association . . . plainly presupposes a freedom not to associate.'"[16] The Court majority found that a major purpose of the Boy Scouts was to instill a certain set of values in its members; and that the Scouts sincerely believed that homosexuality was inconsistent with those values. Ultimately, the Court decided the case on a rule of law vital to a free society: "We are not, as we must not be, guided by our views of whether the Boy Scouts' teachings with respect to homosexual conduct are right or wrong; public or judicial disapproval of an organization's expression does not justify the State's effort to compel the organization to accept members where such acceptance would derogate from the organization's expressive message."[17]

While the Court majority's views in *Dale* certainly are consistent with our constitutional democracy, in which the government is invested with strictly limited powers with the residuum of liberty remaining with the people, the views of three of the justices comprising the *Dale* majority were plainly at odds with their views subsequently expressed in *Lawrence*. In *Dale*, those justices found the public majority's disapproval of discrimination against homosexuality, expressed through democratic processes and interpreted by the state judiciary, to violate the unwritten constitutional protection of expressive association. In *Lawrence*, those same justices found the public majority's disapproval of homosexuality, expressed through democratic processes, to not violate the unwritten constitutional protection of privacy. It is difficult to square their divergent views in the two cases with adherence to a set of consistent constitutional principles, either a presumption in favor of liberty or deference to state sovereignty and democratic processes.

The four liberal dissenters certainly acquitted themselves no better. Despite proclaiming in *Lawrence* that a state's judgments regarding homosexual behavior must yield to the federal constitutional protection of privacy, in *Dale* they found exactly the converse: that the federal constitutional protection of freedom of association must yield to—you guessed it—"the States' right to experiment with 'things social'." By striking down the state's application of the public accommodations law, the dissenters charged, "the Court does not accord this 'courageous State'* the respect that is its due."[18] After all, the dissenters pointed out, "the right to associate for expressive purposes is not . . . absolute."[19] Fortunately for John Lawrence and Tyron Garner, three years later those same justices rediscovered the right to associate, even in a context that some might not find to be "expressive." And fortunately both for the gay couple and the Boy Scouts, Justices O'Connor and Kennedy were prepared to set aside whatever moral proclivi-

---

*As a native New Jerseyan, I've heard a lot of adjectives ascribed to my home state, but not this one.

ties they might have to uphold freedom of association in both cases.

But seven of the nine justices split over the outcome in the two cases, placing the right to be left alone on the shakiest of jurisprudential ground. For the liberal justices, states are free to experiment with social legislation, except when they aren't; free to protect freedom of association for gays, but not for those who choose not to associate with them. For the conservatives, states are free to enact discriminatory morals legislation that intrudes into the sanctity of the home and intimate association, but not to apply antidiscrimination legislation against private organizations. Neither line is philosophically satisfying or consistent.

And, of course, such constitutional zigzagging eviscerates the underlying right, leaving a large swath of individual autonomy susceptible to government intrusion. Never mind the Patriot Act: State and especially local governments, as Madison pointed out more than two centuries ago, are much more inclined to disturb the right of citizens to be left alone. Whether through censorship of books in the public libraries (from either the right or left), through suppression of controversial art exhibits, through meddling social workers intruding upon individual religious beliefs, or through the types of invasions of freedom of association described in this chapter, local governments acting upon the morally inflamed passions of some of its citizens too often act to suppress the right of individuals to pursue happiness as they see fit, even in the most peaceful, private, and intimate ways. And if we abide such intrusions in some instances, we weaken the constraints on government that are designed to protect all of us.

Surely government rightly possesses the power to safeguard the safety and well-being of the community. The balance between individual autonomy and public morality is a delicate one. The more private and nonharmful the conduct, the more protection it deserves. But by allowing the boundaries of government power to be defined not by objective principles informed by a presumption of liberty but by the subjective moral preferences of judges and policymakers, we are in danger of losing our right to be left alone. However nebulous and difficult to define in individual circumstances, that right may be the one Americans truly treasure above all.

8

Racial Discrimination

SCOTT AND LOU ANN MULLEN have their own little melting pot in their household in rural Lexington, Texas. Scott is white, and Lou Ann is Native American. When the Mullens married, they adopted her younger siblings. The family also includes a natural daughter and a biracial adopted daughter along with six other adopted children. Scott and Lou Ann have served as foster parents to a number of children of various races and ethnicities. Their home brims with love and utter devotion to their children.

In 1992, a black baby named Matthew came into the Mullen family as a foster child. Little Matthew, only a few days old, was addicted to crack cocaine and infected with syphilis. The

Mullens painstakingly nursed him to health; and remarkably, by the time he was two years old, he was developmentally on par with other children his age.

Along the way, the Mullens fell in love with the little boy, and decided they wanted to adopt him. When they learned that Matthew had an older brother, Joseph, the Mullens decided they wanted to adopt him, too. They made their intentions known to the Texas Department of Protective and Regulatory Services. The Mullens had an excellent record as foster parents, so they didn't expect any problems. Instead, their hopes were transformed into a living nightmare.

As Lou Ann Mullen recounted, "Several caseworkers [and] the adoption supervisor, they all said 'No, it would be in the kids' best interest to place them in an African American home.' Those words will stick with me for the rest of my life. What about love?"[1]

Matthew was removed from the Mullens' home and placed with his brother in an adoptive home with black parents. Lou Ann recalled the tears that streamed down the entire family's faces the day the little boy was wrenched from the only home he had ever known. The tears returned when Lou Ann discovered Matthew's handprint on the window from which he often would look outside. She refused to clean the window, wanting to keep the handprint as a reminder of their loss, hoping that one day Matthew would be reunited with his true family.

The adoption placement fell apart. But instead of sending Matthew and Joseph to the Mullens' home, they were sent to a home with black foster parents. Meanwhile, Lou Ann experienced the horror and dismay of seeing Matthew advertised on television seeking a loving home.

Texas law at the time forbade discrimination in adoption placements. But social workers contended that they had been "following the law which says that race cannot be the *deter-mining* factor in adoption."[2] It has been my experience that any time race is "one factor," those who favor its use will pry that seemingly benign exception to the rule of nondiscrimination so wide that you can drive a truck through it. "Once one starts down the road of let's wait a little while to find a racially suitable family, that's a very slippery slope," argued Harvard law professor Laurence H. Tribe. "Once you allow the principle that it's O.K. to wait for a short time, there is no principled way to say waiting twice as long is not also O.K."[3]

And indeed that was happening in the area of interracial adoptions. The problem was (and continues to be) a huge statistical mismatch. At the time of the Mullens' struggle, there were 500,000 children in the U.S. foster care system. More than half were minorities, and 40 percent of the total were black. But nationwide, only 13 percent of Americans are black. Moreover, 67 percent of the hard-to-place children were black, while only 31 percent of the waiting families were black.[4]

But for the National Association of Black Social Workers, the issue is not about moving children from foster homes to adoptive families; it's about race. The group considers interracial adoptions "cultural genocide." It would prefer to keep black children in foster homes or orphanages than to allow adoption by nonblack families. But as Harvard law professor Elizabeth Bartholet pointed out, "These policies are seriously harmful to black children. . . . There is not one iota of evidence in all the empirical studies that transracial adoption does any harm at all, compared to same-race adoption. There is plenty of evidence that delay in adoption does do harm."[5]

The resulting system in many instances resembled the Jim Crow era. In Tennessee, a mixed-race child—half black and half white—was considered a black child by the state. But the state considered a mixed-race couple white, with the perverse effect that mixed-race couples were forbidden to adopt children who would appear to be their own biological offspring.

My colleagues and I filed a lawsuit on behalf of the Mullens challenging Texas's racist adoption practices. The issue transcended the ideological divide, and we were joined as co-counsel by Harvard law professors Bartholet, Tribe, and Randall Kennedy.[6] Within days, the agency capitulated and allowed the Mullens to adopt Matthew and Joseph.[7]

The state of Texas strengthened its laws to make discrimination in adoption placements a crime punishable by incarceration. My colleagues and I call it our "send a social worker to jail program." Thereafter, Congress passed a law sponsored by Sen. Howard Metzenbaum (D-OH), the Multiethnic Placement Act of 1994,[8] which forbade discrimination in federally funded adoption placements throughout the country.

Today, Matthew and Joseph Mullen are happy Texas adolescents. But the thought that we as a nation remain so infected by race consciousness that a wonderful family was nearly destroyed by it—and numerous others actually were—is a sobering commentary on where we are in achieving a society that is governed by the principle of racial equality.

This year celebrates the 50th anniversary of *Brown v. Board of Education*[9] and its sacred promise of equal educational opportunities. Who could ever have predicted that half a century after that triumph for equality—and 40 years after the Civil Rights Act of 1964—that Americans would be as divided by race as ever before? Today, individuals' race, color, or ethnicity often determines what jobs are available to them, what district they will be in for voting opportunities, where they can attend school, whether they can get into top colleges or receive scholarships, and the likelihood of whether they will be stopped by police or airport security guards. In many such instances, the government (often state or local or one of their agencies) is engaged in discrimination, in clear violation of the blanket nondiscrimination guarantee of the 14th Amendment.[10]

Too often, one's position on such issues varies according to ideological preferences. Many conservatives will decry racial preferences in college admissions while finding racial profiling entirely permissible; while many liberals see it exactly the reverse. That is one reason why the promise of equality is eroding: Too few of us honor the principle across the board, and too often exceptions to the rule are found. Exceptions that, unfortunately, then serve to sanction the use of discrimination when others find ample justification. In the context of slavery, Thomas Paine argued that it was impossible to compromise equality without destroying it, for whenever we

> depart from the principle of equal rights, or attempt any modification of it, we plunge into a labyrinth of difficulties from which there is no way out but by retreating. Where are we to stop? Or by what principle are we to find out the point to stop at, that shall discriminate between men of the same country, part of whom shall be free, and the rest not?[11]

Paine's warning has proven prophetic repeatedly over the course of American history, from the institution of slavery, to the Jim Crow laws, to the modern forms of state-sanctioned discrimination. Although the federal government has practiced and continues to engage in racial classifications, many of the most egregious violations have occurred at the state and local level. Indeed, it was such discriminatory practices that led to the adoption of the 14th Amendment.[12]

Today, discussions about racial discrimination by government usually revolve around so-called affirmative action or racial profiling. They are not different issues, but two sides of the same discrimination coin. One characteristic shared by all forms of modern discrimination is that race is only "one factor" among many to be considered—but that means, by definition, that at least in some instances it will be the *deciding* factor, as illustrated by the shameful example of barriers to interracial adoption above. Another constant feature of departures from the nondiscrimination principle is that today's beneficiaries of racial preferences can be tomorrow's victims. And still another is that when the use of race by government is permissible under "exigent" circumstances, those circumstances will tend to arise with greater frequency. As Tom Paine urged, whatever the justification, any exception to the absolute principle of equality destroys the rule.

That point was made eloquently by U.S. Supreme Court Justice Tom Jackson in the context of one of the most shameful episodes of racial discrimination in American history, the internment of Japanese Americans during World War II. When the incarceration was challenged, the U.S. Supreme Court upheld it under the government's perceived emergency powers. But Justice Jackson dissented, warning that

> a judicial construction . . . that will sustain this order is a far more subtle blow to liberty than the promulgation of the order itself. . . . [O]nce a judicial opinion rationalizes the Constitution to show that [it] sanctions such an order, the Court for all time has validated the principle of racial discrimination. . . . The principle then lies about like a loaded weapon ready for the hand of any authority that can bring forward a plausible claim of an urgent need.[13]

That proverbial weapon has been fired over and over again, always with tragic consequences.[14]

The inherently perverse effects of racial classifications are exacerbated by the growing phenomenon of multiracialism in the United States. With increasing interracial marriage, children often cannot be placed into easy racial and ethnic categories. One might hope that multiracialism would hasten the day when our governments look at people as Americans, rather than as racially hyphenated groups. Instead, the desire to maintain racial pigeonholes has led public policy along ever more circuitous and arbitrary paths, with the predictable result that racial and ethnic groups increasingly are battling over their share of a racial spoils system.[15]

Most Americans clearly want to remove race from government's policymaking arsenal, even as they support true "affirmative action" for disadvantaged individuals.[16] Outside of the narrow realm of America's elite class, an overwhelming public consensus exists, even among minorities, that merit rather than race should be the sole criterion in hiring, promotion, and college admissions.[17] Voters in California and Washington State approved by lopsided margins initiatives that banned the use of race in public education, employment, and contracts. But in ways reminiscent of the "massive resistance" to federal court desegregation orders in the 1950s and '60s, state and local government officials often refuse to implement voter initiatives and judicial decisions, sometimes blatantly and other times coming up with subtle ways to evade them.

Racial classifications and the ideology that sustains them so permeate public policy at every level of government that officials can be punished for *refusing* to discriminate. Dr. Stanley Dea, a Chinese American, worked his way up the ranks at the Washington Suburban Sanitary Commission in the suburbs surrounding the nation's capital. When he finally earned a supervisory position, he discovered that the commission applied two policies that were hopelessly at odds with each other: a nondiscrimination policy and an affirmative action policy that required the promotion of women and minorities over more-qualified nonminorities. When he learned that the U.S. Supreme Court had forbidden such policies, but that the commission had decided to ignore the ruling, he objected to it. The commission responded by relieving Dea of his supervisory responsibilities.

Represented by private attorney Douglas Herbert and the Institute for Justice, Dea filed a claim of retaliation under the Civil Rights Act of 1964. He was ostracized at the commission, and forced to submit to demeaning working conditions. He suffered a debilitating setback when the federal district court denied his claim. Dea passed away shortly thereafter, unable to witness his vindication in the U.S. Court of Appeals for the Fourth Circuit that had taken 11 years to secure.[18]

Dea's struggle illustrates painfully how far we have strayed in the 40 years since the Civil Rights Act: from an absolute and unequivocal command of nondiscrimination to the threat of official government retaliation for those who dare to stand up for that principle. No wonder that few government officials do dare.

The United States Supreme Court recently had a golden opportunity to strike a vital blow for the principle of equality—but instead, it delivered a mighty blow *against* that principle. Over the past two decades, the Court had been constructing an equal protection jurisprudence that applied the strictest scrutiny to racial classifications created by governments at every level. The Court required that government entities demonstrate a compelling interest—one that could be accomplished only through the narrowly tailored and temporary use of race as a criterion. Racial balancing as an end in itself was completely forsaken. The Court rejected such rationales as the perceived need to provide racial "role models," and found that the only compelling purpose was remedying a governmental entity's own past discrimination; and

RACIAL DISCRIMINATION   133

even then it approved race-conscious remedies only if there
was no alternative.[19] For years, the Supreme Court did not
uphold any racial classifications. Applying the Supreme
Court's precedents, lower federal courts consistently struck
down racial classifications as well. It appeared we were on the
way to embracing as a reality government neutrality toward
race.

That progress all came to a jarring end in two cases challenging racial preferences in admissions policies at the University of Michigan. Advocates of race-based university
admissions policies asserted that there was an exception to
the rule of nondiscrimination. They pointed to the 1978
Bakke decision,[20] in which the swing justice, Lewis Powell,
generally eschewed racial preferences in the university admissions process but endorsed a Harvard affirmative action program that used race as a "plus factor" in admissions.
Contemporary defenders of racial preferences in academia
wielded the *Bakke* precedent along with the mantra of the
supposed academic benefits flowing from racial diversity.

Still, the Supreme Court since *Bakke* repeatedly had indicated in forceful terms that the same strict scrutiny standard
would apply regardless of the context. The hopelessly subjective standard of "diversity" seemingly would be far too nebulous to constitute a "compelling" governmental objective.
Even if the Court accepted the rationale, true diversity could
be far better achieved through consideration of individual
attributes than through the casual and wholesale deployment
of racial stereotypes.

Real-world experience also suggested that racial preferences were not an effective means of redressing the real cause
of racial disparities in college attendance: a large and growing
racial academic gap in K–12 education. Social scientists Stephan and Abigail Thernstrom found that in the late 1980s, the

average black high school senior graduated at a performance level three academic years behind the average white senior. A decade later—in the midst of massive racial preferences in college admissions—that gap had actually *increased* to four academic years.[21] "The truth is that affirmative action is largely irrelevant to increasing minority representation in higher education," argue Jay P. Greene and Greg Forster in a recent *Washington Post* op-ed. "The primary obstacle to getting more minority students into college is that only one in five such students graduate from high school with the bare minimum qualifications needed even to *apply* to four-year colleges." As a result, Greene and Forster conclude, "[u]nless we fix the leaks in the K–12 education pipeline, no higher education policy can possibly improve minority opportunities to attend college."[22]

Not only does the superficial quick fix of racial preferences do nothing to cure the underlying cause of racial disparities in higher education, it actually exacerbates the crisis by creating the illusion that the problem is being solved, when in fact it is growing worse. Race-based affirmative action programs are a form of "trickle-down" civil rights, bestowing most of their benefits on the most-advantaged members of the selected minority groups, while doing nothing to help those at the bottom of the economic or educational ladder.[23]

Moreover, states that abandoned overt racial preferences, due to voter initiatives, court orders, or executive decree, found that there were better ways to increase minority admissions. In the wake of Proposition 209, which abolished racial preferences in California public education, employment, and contracting, the University of California at Berkeley moved toward more-individualized admissions processes and began sending tutors to inner-city schools to boost test scores of economically disadvantaged, mostly minority students.[24] As the

New York Times reported, "ending affirmative action has had one unpublicized and profoundly desirable consequence: it has forced the universit[ies] to try to expand the pool of eligible minority students."[25] Texas and Florida adopted programs that guaranteed admission to all students graduating at the top of their high school classes.[26] But the public universities did not take those steps until the easy out of racial preferences was removed from their policy arsenals.

The existence of such less-burdensome alternatives seemed to seal the constitutional fate of programs—like those employed by the University of Michigan—that overtly used racial preferences. And indeed the Court, by a 6-3 vote,[27] did strike down the university's rigid preferences in undergraduate admissions, where each minority candidate automatically received 20 points on a 150-point scale.[28] (By contrast, an outstanding personal essay was worth only 3 points, and only 5 points were awarded for personal achievement, leadership, or public service.[29])

But by a 5-4 margin, the Court approved the more subtle, yet still massive, use of race at the University of Michigan law school.[30] That challenge was filed by Barbara Grutter, a white woman who applied to the law school with a 3.6 undergraduate grade-point average and a 161 score on the Law School Admission Test. While Grutter was not admitted, black and Hispanic students with far lesser academic credentials were.

The law school acknowledged that the admissions process was designed to achieve a "critical mass" of minority students—a goal no one could define with precision—and that race could be a determinative factor.[31] While the Court's majority purported to apply strict constitutional scrutiny, its actual analysis fell far short of that exacting standard. Far from demanding a compelling purpose, the Court's majority stated that the "Law School's educational judgment that such diversity is essential to its educational mission is one to which we defer."[32] The Court dispensed with the narrow tailoring requirement as well. While public universities "cannot establish quotas for members of certain racial groups or put members of those groups on separate admissions tracks," the Court declared, they "can, however, consider race or ethnicity more flexibly as a 'plus' factor in the context of individualized consideration of each and every applicant."[33] Soothing words; but in practical consequence, a distinction without a difference. The undergraduate school was a bit more honest about its techniques, but the end result—and the massive preferences utilized to attain it—was essentially the same. Whether "flexible" or rote, racial discrimination is still discrimination, and any exception to the principle of nondiscrimination inevitably swallows the rule.

All of which the four dissenters pointed out.[34] Justice Kennedy declared that the Court did "not apply strict scrutiny. By trying to say otherwise, it undermines both the test and its own controlling precedents."[35] He derided the concept of critical mass, which is "a delusion used by the Law School to mask its attempt to make race an automatic factor in most instances and to achieve numerical goals indistinguishable from quotas." The Court's abandonment of principle, he argued, could have devastating consequences. "Preferment by race, when resorted to by the State," Kennedy proclaimed, "can be the most divisive of all policies, containing within it the potential to destroy confidence in the Constitution and in the idea of equality."[36]

Justice Clarence Thomas highlighted the huge racial credentials gap among law school applicants: Although blacks constitute 11.1 percent of those applying to law schools, they account for only 1.1 percent of applicants who score 165 or higher on the LSAT.[37] As a consequence, he charged, the

"Law School takes unprepared students with the promise of a University of Michigan degree and all of the opportunities that it offers. Those overmatched students take the bait, only to find that they cannot succeed in the cauldron of competition."[38] Moreover, "the Law School's racial discrimination does nothing for those too poor or uneducated to participate in elite higher education and therefore presents only an illusory solution to the challenges facing our Nation."[39] Ultimately, Thomas concluded that the "Constitution abhors classifications based on race, not only because those classifications can harm favored races or are based on illegitimate motives, but also because every time the government places citizens on racial registers and makes race relevant to the provision of burdens or benefits, it demeans us all."[40]

For the majority, Justice O'Connor remarked that "[w]e take the Law School at its word that it would 'like nothing better than to find a race-neutral admissions formula' and will terminate its race-conscious admissions program as soon as practicable"[41] — an assertion that is almost laughable considering the persistence and ubiquitousness of racial preferences in university admissions. She added, "We expect that 25 years from now, the use of racial preferences will no longer be necessary to further the interest approved today."[42] Unfortunately, the impact of the Court's decision will be to delay the day of reckoning over the racial achievement gap, therefore decreasing the likelihood that racial disparities will disappear. In the meantime, as Justice Thomas quipped, the Court granted "a 25-year license to violate the Constitution."[43] And the murky rationale on which the decision rests easily could seep out into other areas of public policy, giving government-imposed racial classifications a new lease on life.

Racial classifications in the name of diversity infect not only university admissions, but school assignments at the

K–12 level as well. The bizarre yet all-too-predictable effects of such social engineering played out in Montgomery County, Maryland, which like many school districts uses race to determine admission into elite, specialized "magnet" schools. In 1995, the parents of Eleanor Glewwe and Hana Maruyama decided to remove their children from Takoma Park Elementary School and enroll them in a French immersion program at Maryvale Elementary School in Rockville. Both Eleanor and Hana had one white and one Asian American parent. Because the school district forces parents to choose a category for their children, the girls were classified as Asian.

The school district rejected their applications because there were too few Asian children already at Takoma Park, and the girls' departure would further reduce that number. "It's painful to hear you cannot get into one of the programs Montgomery County is famous for just because you're Asian," complained Warren Maruyama, Hana's dad. "It's clear what you have here is a thinly disguised system of racial quotas."

Don't worry, school officials told the disappointed parents: just reclassify the girls as white and apply again. There weren't too few white students at Takoma Park, so leaving shouldn't be a problem.

Eleanor's mother did just that—but the application was denied again. This time, the problem was that there were *too many* whites at Maryvale, so their transfer would adversely alter the racial balance in the receiving school.[44]

Eventually, the girls were allowed to transfer, but only after exposés in the *Washington Post* and on *CBS Evening News*.[45] The notion that the educational opportunities of a child of mixed ancestry depend on which racial category he or she checks is all too reminiscent of the case of Adolph Plessy, who was denied admission to a railway car because he was one-eighth black. Can it be that we have traveled so far and painful a distance over the past century only to end up in the same place we started?

Children like Eleanor and Hana should not be sacrificed at the altar of racial discrimination, whether the euphemism is "separate but equal" or "diversity." America is not about redistribution of opportunities on the basis of race. It is about expanding opportunities, so that every individual, regardless of race, is ensured a chance to strive and risk and achieve to the limits of his or her abilities.

If we have learned anything since our nation's founding, it is that the results of racial classifications ultimately are never benevolent. For every beneficiary there is a victim. Today's winners can be tomorrow's losers. And even those who seem to benefit are made worse off by the corrosive effects of unearned gains.

The problem exists at every level of government, but at the state and local levels racial preferences are especially pervasive. The concept of equal protection of the laws cannot long abide arbitrary racial classifications. As a nation, we need to decide which we value more: our cherished constitutional values or a racial system that divides Americans on the most invidious of grounds. When empowered to do so, Americans invariably choose to vindicate the values that make us free. Unfortunately, government too often refuses to listen, thereby perpetuating a particularly vexing and demoralizing form of grassroots tyranny that should long ago have been consigned to a richly deserved demise.

Perhaps racial preferences will collapse under the weight of their own illogic, as ethnic groups battle one another for an ever-bigger share of racial entitlements, often for the wealthiest members in the name of the most-disadvantaged. Personally, I think it already has reached that point: Recently a middle-class, mixed-race member of my own family qualified for a race-based affirmative action program and eagerly took advantage of it. Put another way, in the government's eyes, my sibling's marriage to a non-Caucasian rendered their children disadvantaged—a transformation that seems more than a bit condescending and tinged with notions of ethnic inferiority. That a member of the Bolick family—which has been in America for more than 200 years—qualified for race-based affirmative action demonstrates that the whole racial classification enterprise is certifiably insane.

9

The
Government
School System

IN JUNE 1994, a high school graduation ceremony was held in a Bethlehem, Pennsylvania Unitarian Church for two local schoolchildren, Lynn Steirer and David Moralis. The two seniors could not join their classmates at the regular graduation festivities at Liberty High School—a school whose name turns out to be quite a misnomer—not because they dropped out, or took drugs, or failed final exams. They were prevented from graduating because as a matter of conscience they refused to submit to their school's mandatory community service program.

"I think that volunteering is a good thing to do," explained Lynn Steirer. "But volunteering is doing something of your own free will, and out of the kindness of your heart, not because someone forces you to do it."

At the same time, Chapel Hill, North Carolina, honor student Aric Herndon was learning that the hundreds of hours he spent volunteering through the Boy Scouts would not count toward his high school's mandatory community service requirements because he was "compensated" for it by earning Eagle Scout honors.

Meanwhile, in Maryland, which has statewide mandatory community service requirements championed by former Lieutenant Governor Kathleen Kennedy Townsend, the state devised a chart depicting the hierarchy of possible community service activities—with "lobbying" at the very top.

"Compulsory volunteerism" is the latest oxymoronic fad sweeping public schools across the nation. As of the mid-1990s, approximately one-third of all government schools required community service as a condition of graduation. While no one can contest that volunteerism is noble, the question is in what realm it belongs: individual autonomy or government coercion. An aspect of life that previously was left to the discretion of parents and students—often as a matter of religious conscience—is now becoming a matter of government compulsion in school districts around the nation, which dictate when, where, and how much time students will volunteer, and which activities will count toward the requirement. So far, the federal courts have declined to strike down the programs as a violation of parental autonomy.[1]

As political institutions, government school systems often reflect the values of powerful interest groups. A few years ago, self-esteem was all the rage. The principal of one of my sons' schools told me that the school had two objectives: to impart learning and to make the students feel good about themselves. No, I replied; if you do the first part right, the second will follow. Instead, by defining their objectives in that man-

ner, the schools can be assured of meeting half of their objectives: kids who may not be able to read or write but nonetheless possess tremendous self-esteem. As if to confirm that
fear, a teacher recently told me not to worry about my son's
deplorable spelling, because "we don't really do spelling any-
more." The whole situation seems head-spinningly Orwellian
to me, but at least I can take action about it. I can only imagine
how parents fare who, unlike me, don't sue bureaucrats and
specialize in education issues for a living.

While government schools are spending resources doing
things they shouldn't be doing, their track record is far worse
when it comes to fulfilling their essential goal of providing the
educational basics. Many parents in the suburbs are vaguely
aware of the problem, particularly when standardized tests
reveal vast numbers of failing students (which usually is followed by demands not to fix the problem but to get rid of the
tests). But the reality is most grim in large urban school districts across the nation, where children in public schools face
a much greater likelihood of lives in poverty or crime than of
going on to higher education or productive livelihoods.

I gained my perspective on this subject in the trenches,
having litigated education issues in inner-city school districts
for more than a decade.[2] My efforts involving the Cleveland
public schools culminated in a 2003 Supreme Court decision
upholding the Cleveland school choice program.[3] During that
litigation battle, the phrase "one in fourteen" haunted my psy-
che. A child in the Cleveland public schools had slightly less
than a one-in-fourteen chance of graduating on time with
senior-level proficiency. The same child had slightly less than
a one-in-fourteen chance of being a victim of crime, inside the
schools, each year. In Milwaukee, whose school choice program I litigated during most of the 1990s, the typical child in
the public schools had less than a 50-50 chance of graduating.

For children from families on public assistance, the odds declined to 15 percent.

When similar numbers are replicated elsewhere—as they are in many large inner-city government school systems—we have a serious national crisis on our hands. For that reason, we should not be worrying whether particular reform proposals are too radical. We should be worrying whether they are radical enough.

Our nation's public school system as a whole is not doing a particularly good job in accomplishing its mission of providing basic educational skills to America's schoolchildren. Whether compared with other industrialized nations or measured against state or national standards, our public schools often produce dismal, sometimes embarrassing, results. Foreigners flock to the United States for our postsecondary system of education; but few come except from third-world countries for our K–12 schools. Not coincidentally, America's postsecondary schools are characterized by competition and choice: Students can use government grants or loans at any school they choose, public or private. But our K–12 system of public schools, by contrast, represents perhaps the largest socialized delivery system outside of Communist China. And the results are all too predictable.

Many conservatives cling nostalgically to the notion of "local control" of education. And indeed, local control unquestionably is vastly preferable to national control. Given that the consumers of education are children, and no two children's educational needs are the same, it makes sense that educational services should be as decentralized as possible. But local school boards, particularly in large urban school districts, provide perhaps the greatest example of the inefficiencies and dysfunctions of any governmental entities in the United States, exemplifying vividly and painfully the prescience of James Madison's warnings about the negative propensities of local governments. Many local school districts are controlled by self-interested political pressure groups—namely, the people they employ. As a result, the educational interests of the children often are sacrificed to political expediency. The schools operate as a monopoly, sheltered from the market consequences of failure. As indicated in chapter 1, over the past several decades there has been enormous consolidation of school districts across the United States, making them even more bureaucratic and resistant to reform than before. And because they are governmental institutions, public schools are subject to every passing political fad that gains currency among the political elite.

Nor do most popular reform proposals hold much promise. In their most recent book, *No Excuses*, Abigail and Stephan Thernstrom examine nearly every reform that has been tested in government education in recent years, from smaller class sizes to increased funding to accountability measures.[4] They found that apart from modest gains attributable to increased standards in states such as Texas and North Carolina, few reforms show much promise. Moreover, the system's ability to adopt and respond to meaningful reform is paralyzed by special interests who have a powerful interest in preserving the status quo. The Thernstroms characterize the racial gap as "the most important civil rights issue of our time," and urge that the "nation's system of education must be fundamentally altered, with real educational choice as part of the package."[5]

Those who suffer the most are typically the same children who need education the most: youngsters from economically disadvantaged families;[6] this manifests itself in large racial disparities in student achievement. As touched upon in the preceding chapter, the academic gap between white and

Asian students on the one hand and black and Hispanic students on the other is gaping and growing. The 2000 National Assessment of Educational Progress, for instance, revealed that a shocking 63 percent of black fourth-graders and 56 percent of their Hispanic counterparts scored below the most basic level of reading proficiency.[7] On a recent Scholastic Aptitude Test, 10 percent of all testees scored at least 1300 (out of 1600 points), the usual minimum cut-off for many elite institutions of higher education. But only 1.5 percent of black testees — or 1,877 nationwide — scored 1300 or higher. Nationally, 13,897 testees scored 1500 or higher on the SAT. Only 72 black testees in the entire country scored that high.[8] The national graduation rate in the public high school class of 2000 was 69 percent; but for black students it was only 55 percent, and 53 percent for Hispanics.[9] For many children of color, the promise of equal educational opportunities issued a half-century ago in *Brown v. Board of Education* has proven illusory.

While wealthier families have the ability to move to communities with better public school systems* or send their children to private schools, low-income families usually do not. Their children typically are consigned to dangerous, poor-quality, inner-city schools in large urban school districts where, unlike in suburbia, parents have little influence over their children's fate.

It was not supposed to be this way. Under our constitutional system, parents — not the state — are entrusted with the primary role in the education of their children. A century ago, nativists attempted to homogenize public schools and restrict

---

*Federal tax policy supports such choices. When families move to more expensive communities in order to avail themselves of better public schools, they may deduct both their higher mortgage interest and local property taxes from their federal income tax.

educational options. The Ku Klux Klan helped persuade Oregon to require all children to attend government schools. The U.S. Supreme Court struck down the law because it "unreasonably interferes with the liberty of parents and guardians to direct the upbringing and education of children," declaring unequivocally:

> The fundamental theory of liberty upon which all governments in this Union repose excludes any power of the State to standardize its children by forcing them to accept instruction from public teachers only. The child is not the mere creature of the State; those who nurture him and direct his destiny have the right, coupled with the high duty, to recognize and prepare him for additional obligations.[10]

Today, real parental choice in most states is nonexistent, as bureaucrats have supplanted parents and teachers as the primary determinants of the educational fate of children. And again, the less economic or political clout parents have, the less influence they will have over their children's education.

The consequences of that inverted power structure were probed insightfully by two educational scholars, John E. Chubb and Terry M. Moe, in a pathbreaking 1990 study for the Brookings Institution titled *Politics, Markets & America's Schools*.[11] They set out to answer an intriguing question: Why are inner-city government schools so shockingly bad, while inner-city private schools and suburban public schools generally do a decent job? They found that although student ability and family background are important factors in student achievement, school organization also plays an important role. Specifically, they determined that over a four-year high school experience, effectively organized schools "increase the achievement of [their] students by more than one full year" as compared to ineffectively organized schools.[12] What makes a school more or less effective? Chubb and Moe found that common denominators among effective schools were a clear mission, strong leadership, autonomy for principals and teachers, and parental choice. They observed that large inner-city government school systems are characterized by massive bureaucracies that make it difficult for principals to lead, for teachers to teach, for parents to exert influence, and for reform to take hold.

Moreover, Chubb and Moe found that urban public school systems, in particular, are especially sensitive to special-interest manipulation. All government school districts are susceptible to such influences because they are by their nature political institutions. As such, they are answerable not to the consumers they serve—parents and children—but to politicians. In turn, the groups that are influential in the local political process, especially teachers' unions, tend to dominate policy. In school board elections, which usually experience notoriously low voter turnouts, groups like unions can dominate the process. The school board in turn hires school district officials. When it comes time to negotiate over contracts, the unions often end up negotiating with themselves. And the entire system, not surprisingly, is decidedly resistant to reform. The situation is exacerbated in large urban districts whose sheer size makes them unreceptive to the concerns of individual parents, and whose nominal constituents (the parents) lack the ability to pick up and move their children elsewhere.

By contrast, parents in suburban school districts have clout because they possess the means to move their children elsewhere, which would deprive the school district of the per-pupil resources allocated for those children. That financial consequence makes bureaucrats take notice. Similarly, in private schools, which are fully dependent for their survival on satisfied parents, the consumer reigns supreme. For that reason, Chubb and Moe concluded that the availability of educational choices, especially for poor parents, is a vital prerequisite for educational reform and improvement.

Chubb and Moe's findings are borne out in the real world. I'll never forget statistics that I learned when litigating a school choice lawsuit in Chicago in the early 1990s. At the time, the Chicago public schools had roughly 400,000 students and 3,200 bureaucrats. Chicago Catholic schools, by contrast, had about 100,000 students and 40 administrators. Hence the ratio of public school students to private school students was about 4:1, whereas the ratio of public school administrators to private school administrators was 80:1. When the low-income parents I represented were asked why they didn't try to improve the system from within, they spoke of the difficulty of influencing a massive bureaucracy warehoused in an old Army barracks on Pershing Road in an isolated section of the city. Chicago's situation is not an aberration: In many large urban school districts, 50 cents out of every educational dollar is siphoned off before it ever reaches the classroom. That is why school districts like Newark, New Jersey are spending upwards of $14,000 per student with hardly anything to show for it in terms of student achievement.

Meaningful education reform requires what I call "the three Ds": deregulation, decentralization, and depoliticization. Government schools should be unshackled so that each individual school has control over its curriculum and programs—in other words, as former president Bill Clinton once advocated, all schools should be charter schools. Funding should be student-centered. Except perhaps for capital expenditures, funding should come not through the decrees of a central bureaucracy, but through the student, with an equal amount allocated for each child. School districts would evolve from central political command structures into service providers, allocating resources that have significant economies of scale, such as special services for disabled children.

Such a system would be highly responsive to the particularized needs of individual children. The concept of one size fits all, reflected in today's homogenized and politicized curricula in which each regular public school in a district is likely doing the same thing at the same time as every other school, does not work. Indeed, student-based educational funding would allow children to choose from a menu of educational services—from computer-based education to private or public schooling to tutoring or special services. A school's success would depend largely upon satisfying parents. The focus would be on educational basics, rather than on passing educational fancies. And such a structure would largely eliminate special-interest pressure over education.

In sketching a system along those lines,[13] Chubb and Moe observe that the "crucial difference" between the current system and one characterized by school autonomy and parental choice is that "most of those who previously held authority over the schools would have their authority permanently withdrawn, and that authority would be vested in schools, parents, and children."[14] They argue, "There is nothing in the concept of democracy to require that schools be subject to direct control by school boards, central offices, departments of education, and other arms of government. . . . There are many paths of democracy and public education." Displacing the current top-down, command-and-control system of education with a system characterized by school autonomy and parental choice, they conclude, is necessary "to get to the root of the problem."[15]

The single most important reform element in moving toward such a system is parental choice. In April 2004, I joined the newly created Alliance for School Choice as its president and general counsel to help further the cause of parental choice. Fortunately, we are moving in that direction, albeit at a seemingly glacial pace.[16] Most states have adopted some form of deregulated charter public schools, though they still comprise only a small fraction of the overall national student population. Some states have created public-school choice and open enrollment programs. A few pathbreaking states, such as Wisconsin, Ohio, Florida, and Colorado, have adopted programs that allow children who come from disadvantaged families or who attend failing government schools to choose private schools. Others, including Arizona, Illinois, Florida, and Pennsylvania have enacted tax credits for private school tuition or scholarships. At the national level, the No Child Left Behind Act requires school districts to make alternatives available to children in failing government schools, though such options are woefully inadequate[17] and the promise apparently is not legally enforceable by parents and children. Most recently, in 2004, Congress enacted and President George W. Bush signed into law a pilot school choice program for children in the dysfunctional District of Columbia Public Schools.

But such systemic reforms are resisted tenaciously by public school officials and their reactionary allies, the National Education Association, the American Federation of Teachers, People for the American Way, the American Civil Liberties Union, the National Association for the Advancement of Colored People, and others. That is the lesson that Wisconsin State Rep. Polly Williams learned when she pioneered the nation's first urban school choice program in 1990. The program was a modest experiment, limited initially to 1 percent of the Milwaukee Public Schools' students, who could use the state share of their public school funding as full payment of tuition in participating nonsectarian private schools.

In the first year of the program, during the 1990–91 school year, fewer than one thousand schoolchildren and a dozen private schools participated in the program. Yet the education establishment reacted as if a bomb had been set off. Not only did the teachers' union file a lawsuit challenging the program's constitutionality, but the superintendent of public instruction—a man who, ironically, had two *Sesame Street* names, Bert Grover—tried to sentence the program to death by bureaucratic strangulation by imposing a blizzard of regulations on the private schools.

Working with Rep. Williams, I represented low-income parents who intervened to defend the program and challenge the regulations. Recognizing that education was essential to give their children a chance to lift themselves out of poverty, the parents were desperate to get their children out of failing schools and into good ones. Pilar Gomez typified the spirit of the parents. "I will find a way to have my children attend private school even if it means less food on the table," she declared. "A quality education for my children is that important."[18]

The parents traveled by bus from Milwaukee to Madison, Wisconsin, for a Saturday court hearing in the middle of August, 1990. Wearing red, white, and blue school choice buttons, they bore silent testimony to how much was at stake. Arrayed against an army of government officials and special-interest lawyers, they made for a classic David versus Goliath battle. But David won, when Judge Susan Steingass upheld the constitutionality of the school choice program and struck down most of Grover's rules.[19]

That decision was upheld two years later by the Wiscon-

sin Supreme Court. Justice Louis Ceci captured the importance of the program:

> Literally thousands of school children in the Milwaukee
> public school system have been doomed because of those in
> government who insist upon maintaining the status quo.
> . . . The Wisconsin legislature, attuned and attentive to the
> seemingly insurmountable problems confronting socioeco-
> nomically deprived children, has attempted to throw a life
> preserver to those Milwaukee schoolchildren caught in the
> cruel riptide of a school system floundering upon the shoals
> of poverty, status-quo thinking, and despair.[20]

The Milwaukee school choice program performed well,
expanding substantially in the mid-1990s to encompass as
many as 15,000 children and to include religious schools
among the educational options. Not only did the students who
were able to move to private schools do well, but the competitive pressure from the choice program forced the Milwaukee
Public Schools to improve and adopt long-overdue reforms.
Still, intransigent government officials and their special-
interest allies continue to try to stymie the program.

That same potent political combination has thwarted
school choice in most other states; and where it has been
enacted, it inevitably has led to legal challenges.[21] Eventually,
following a court hearing outside of which hundreds of low-
income parents and children gathered from all around the
nation to demonstrate their support for school choice, the
U.S. Supreme Court ruled 5-4 to uphold the Cleveland program and to lift the federal constitutional cloud that had hov-
ered over the nation's most promising education reform. As
Justice Clarence Thomas declared, "Today many of our inner-
city schools deny emancipation to urban minority students,"
who "have been forced into a system that continually fails
them."[22] He observed, "While the romanticized ideal of uni-

versal public education resonates with the cognoscenti who oppose vouchers, poor urban families just want the best education for their children, who will certainly need it to function in our high-tech and advanced society."[23]

Those battles are far from over. The teachers' unions have reached into what National Education Association general counsel calls their "bag of tricks" to invoke state constitutional provisions in their effort to block school choice. School choice programs in Florida and Colorado, aimed at helping children in failing public schools, are mired in state constitutional litigation bankrolled by the teachers' unions and their allies. The battle to transform the American educational landscape through parental choice will be a long and difficult one. But if we are to finally vindicate the unfulfilled promise of equal educational opportunities, prying the governance of our schools away from self-interested government bureaucrats is essential.

Public education is the most important function of state and local government, arguably even more than police protection. Indeed, police resources are strained in large measure precisely because our schools so often have failed. Public schools consume a vastly disproportionate percentage of taxpayer expenditures, with an insatiable demand for more. Yet they have done both far too much and far too little, operating as bastions of political correctness even as they frequently fail at their core mission. Only through decentralizing authority to the level of schools, teachers, and parents; only by directing funding not to institutions as ends in themselves but to the system's intended beneficiaries; only by returning control over basic educational decisions to the people with the greatest stake in success—the parents—will we ever have an educational system of which we can be proud. That day cannot come quickly enough.

PART THREE

Taming
the Beast

10

Fighting Big Government at the Local Level

IT WAS NOT supposed to be this way, with state and local governments running roughshod over individual liberties. Whatever the nostalgic apologists for "states' rights" might contend, state and local governments were intended to be the guardians of individual liberty, not its assailants. Likewise, state and federal courts were supposed to ensure that governments at every level were restricted to the appropriate boundaries of power, rather than indulging presumptions in favor of the exercise of government power.

As the preceding pages chronicle, James Madison's warning 225 years ago could have been penned today: "The legislative department is everywhere extending the sphere of its

activity and drawing all power into its impetuous vortex."
Madison urged that it is therefore "against the enterprising
ambition of this department that the people ought to indulge
all their jealousy and exhaust all their precautions."[1] Sage
advice in 21st-century America.

The framers, of course, constructed precisely the constitutional safeguards that Madison and his compatriots urged
for the security of liberty. And for a time, and to an extent,
they worked. Until the early 20th century, legislators spent
much of their time debating not only the substance of proposed legislation, but whether they possessed the requisite
authority to enact such legislation in the first place. Indeed,
the 14th Amendment itself was adopted due to congressional
concerns and presidential warnings about congressional
power to enact civil rights protections. Today, legislators
rarely question their authority to enact legislation regarding
almost any matter.

Likewise, state and federal courts traditionally examined
carefully whether legitimate governmental authority existed
to curtail the exercise of individual liberty.[2] Since the 1930s,
in most contexts courts instantly presume the government's
authority and presume constitutionality of laws and regulations.[3]

How can we rein in rapacious government? It would be
nice if we had elected officials who understood that in a free
society, there are limits to the proper exercise of government
powers—and if we had elected officials who abided those limits. Likewise, Americans in general are responsible for our
own calamity, for not only do we not insist on government
leaders who respect the limits of authority, but too often we
demand that government solve all manner of problems it is
not equipped to address, or, even worse, that it manipulate
the burdens and benefits of life to our personal advantage.

Such is human nature, whose excesses our republican form of government is supposed to curb.

If the elected branches of government are unlikely to adequately safeguard liberty, where can we turn? For better or worse, the main recourse is the courts.

It is true that courts themselves too often have been the handmaidens of big government, ushering in welfare entitlements, racial preferences, and the like. Only relatively recently have principled activists in the freedom movement turned their attention to the courts, and the results by and large have been encouraging. There are two types of judicial activism: where the courts exceed the judicial power and take on executive or legislative powers, and create new rights or entitlements unknown to the Constitution; and a second, even worse variety, where courts refuse to enforce rights that are in the Constitution. We have made important strides in recent years curbing both types of judicial activism; and if those trends are to continue, we must play an active role in the advocacy process.

Some might argue that recourse to judicial intervention is profoundly undemocratic. To the contrary, the courts in a republican form of government are an essential *part* of the democratic process, for they act to constrain the inherent democratic impulse toward larger government and the invasion of individual rights. That is not to say that courts always do perform that democratic checking function, but rather that they should. Moreover, for better or worse, courts are our best hope in reestablishing some firm tethers on the exercise of government power.

As my colleague Steve Simpson puts it,

> That the problem of faction still exists today, despite the framers' efforts to avoid it, should serve as a warning sign.

Something has gone wrong in our constitutional system.
Courts bear a large part of the responsibility. They have
allowed government to grow far beyond its intended size
and scope. With government doing as much as it does
today, the opportunities for abuse are many. If courts are
not going to limit the size of government, they must be prepared at the very least to limit its abuses. Yet they cannot
discharge this vital responsibility if they refuse to judge.[4]

And, of course, courts cannot judge unless we ask them
to. To eradicate grassroots tyranny, we must become ever
more active in the courts, advocating creatively and persua-
sively to reestablish proper boundaries of government power.

When I speak of action to protect liberty in the courts, I
mean three types of courts: federal courts, state courts, and
the court of public opinion. I will address each of those outlets in turn.

Federal Courts

If the purpose of the 14th Amendment can be summed up in
one phrase, it would be this: to enlist the national government, and in particular the federal courts, in the eradication
of grassroots tyranny. As described in the early chapters, the
libertarian framers of the 14th Amendment understood that
the Constitution had one major structural deficiency: that
state and local governments were not adequately constrained
in their propensity to violate the constitutional rights of their
own people. So the federal courts were called upon to create
a check upon that propensity.

Sometimes they do, and too often they do not. But freedom advocates will find within our national constitution an
array of protections of individual rights and restraints on the
power of government that can be wielded against local tyr-

anny. Some are tried and true, such as the First Amendment's guarantees of freedom of speech and religion. Others, such as the privileges or immunities clause and the prohibition against impairment of contracts, are badly in need of revival.

A good example of how to effectively litigate against grassroots tyranny in the federal courts is the campaign to restore economic liberty as a fundamental civil right.[5] When I filed my first case in this area in 1987, economic liberty was a jurisprudential wasteland. As described in chapter 4, the U.S. Supreme Court had not struck down a regulation of entry into a business or profession under the 14th Amendment in about 50 years. The keys to reversing that trend were two: finding the right legal theories and finding the right case.

As discussed earlier, economic liberty was intended to be protected under the privileges or immunities clause of the 14th Amendment. But given the overwhelming weight of adverse precedents, no lower federal court would seriously entertain a privileges or immunities claim against an economic regulation. The vindication of the privileges or immunities clause and overturning of the dreaded *Slaughter-House Cases* would be the long-range jurisprudential goal of the economic liberty campaign; but until that day occurred, we would have to find more viable legal theories.

For the moment, the strongest arguments seemed to be the equal protection and due process guarantees of the 14th Amendment. In some instances, the courts had invalidated local laws that divided opportunities on the basis of arbitrary lines.[6] And in others, courts had struck down laws in which the rules governing access to opportunities were hopelessly skewed. It was upon those slender reeds that we would attempt to construct a jurisprudence of economic liberty.

In finding the right first case, I hoped to find an outrageous barrier to economic opportunity that it would be all but impossible for the government to defend. I found it in the pages of the *Washington Post Magazine*, in the person of a man whose name seemed to belong in an Ayn Rand novel: Ego Brown.

In the mid-1980s, Brown had been a bureaucrat toiling for the U.S. Navy. But he always had aspired to operate a business of his own. He discovered his niche in the thousands of scuffed shoes pounding the pavement in the nation's capital.

Brown quit his job and invested in an elegant street-corner shoeshine stand, which he erected at the busy corner of 19th and M Streets. He bought a tuxedo that would become his trademark, and aided by a flamboyant personality, began offering the "Ego Shine" to passersby.

The business was so popular that he decided to expand. But there wasn't enough of a margin to employ his own staff. So naturally, he decided to franchise. But not just to anyone: His franchisees came from the ranks of the homeless, to whom he offered a tuxedo, a shoeshine stand, training, and a chance to lift themselves out of poverty. Brown's efforts were so successful that social workers began referring enterprising homeless people to him.

But in the District of Columbia, it seems no good deed goes unpunished. District police officers dusted off an old Jim Crow–era law, designed to keep blacks from achieving economic emancipation, that forbade shoeshine stands on public streets. One could sell hot dogs, flowers, or photo opportunities with cardboard politicians, but not a shoeshine.

Ego Brown was my first client as a public-interest lawyer. Together we challenged the ban on street-corner shoeshine stands. The District's lawyers refused to provide *any* rationale for the law, maintaining that they need not do so under applicable constitutional precedents. As a result, the federal district court struck down the law as a violation of equal protection. "A court would be shirking its most basic duty," the court declared, "if it abstained from both an analysis of the legislation's articulated objective and the method that the legislature employed to achieve that objective." Applying the test, the court concluded that "we would have to 'strain our imagination' to justify prohibiting bootblacks from the use of public space while permitting access to virtually every other type of vendor."[7]

The *Brown* decision became the building block for other favorable economic liberty decisions, providing courts a rationale by which to apply a means/ends analysis to measure whether constraints on marketplace entry either serve nefarious objectives or are excessive in their scope. Applying that framework, a federal district court in Texas struck down Houston's anti-jitney law on behalf of entrepreneur Alfredo Santos, who wanted to start a jitney commuter service using his off-duty taxicab. The ordinance was enacted in 1905 when streetcar companies lobbied to outlaw their jitney competitors. "The purpose of the law was protectionism in its most glaring form," declared Judge John Rainey. "The ordinance has long outlived its ill-begotten existence."[8]

Since then, my colleagues and I have successfully litigated challenges against California's cosmetology law on behalf of African hairstylists[9] and against Tennessee's casket monopoly.[10] We have a long way to go before economic liberty routinely receives the judicial protection it deserves and was intended to have. Indeed, full protection for economic liberty likely will necessitate the U.S. Supreme Court overturning the *Slaughter-House Cases*. But these jurisprudential baby steps, taken with strategically selected cases featuring sympathetic clients and outrageous restraints on economic liberty, are slowly but surely rebuilding the legal foundations for the revival of a fundamental but often-forgotten civil right. Freedom advocates should employ similar tactics in other areas to protect individual liberty against grassroots tyranny.

State Constitutions

State constitutions, not the federal constitution, were intended to provide the main protection for individual liberty. But for all the talk among conservatives and libertarians about federalism, most freedom advocates think instinctively — sometimes exclusively — in terms of federal court litigation in protecting individual liberty. Federal court litigation provides the potential benefit of more broadly applicable precedents. But state constitutions present a largely untapped treasure trove in terms of restraints on the power of state and local governments and protections for individual liberty.*

Liberal activists discovered the potential of state constitutions decades ago. The key legal principle at work in such litigation is that although the national constitution provides the *floor* for the protection of individual rights, state courts may construe their own constitutions to go *above and beyond* those protections. In more than a dozen states, for instance, liberal activists have succeeded in convincing state courts to construe their own constitutions to guarantee a fundamental right to education and to require some equality of spending.[11] Expansive tort liability, greater protections for criminal defendants, and the right to gay marriage are all examples of

*For precisely that reason, the Institute for Justice in 2001 began opening state chapters to supplement its national litigation agenda by focusing exclusively on litigating under state constitutions to combat grassroots tyranny at its source. IJ's first two state chapters are in Phoenix and Seattle. I drew the hardship duty of moving from Washington, DC, to Phoenix to open the first chapter and direct the overall state chapters project from 2001 to 2004.

results liberal activists have obtained through strategic litigation under state constitutions.

Freedom advocates have been slower to discover and litigate strategically under state constitutions, but the potential is boundless. State constitutions are libertarian nirvana.

One major difference between federal and state litigation is access to the courts. "Standing" to sue in federal courts is severely circumscribed, even if a law is blatantly unconstitutional. Taxpayers generally do not have standing under the federal constitution; rather, plaintiffs attempting to challenge a law in federal court must demonstrate a discrete, particularized injury that the public at large does not sustain in equal measure. Likewise, some issues are deemed "political questions" that can only be resolved by the elected branches of government. For example, taxpayers generally cannot challenge federal spending programs even if they exceed the proper boundaries of congressional power.

By contrast, most state courts freely confer standing upon taxpayers to challenge almost any unconstitutional exercise of government power. That is why, for instance, taxpayers can challenge the building of sports arenas under state constitutions. Likewise, while federal courts presume the constitutionality of governmental decision making, under most state constitutions, municipalities are strictly limited to powers expressly provided by state law. So if a local government cannot point to an express source of power, a state court will strike down an enactment on the principle of *ultra vires* (i.e., it is outside the government's corporate power).

But best of all are express provisions in state constitutions that limit government power or protect individual liberty that often go far beyond similar provisions in their federal counterpart. Remember that just as with the U.S. Constitution, constitutions in the original states often were written by statesmen who were deeply imbued in the principles of liberty. Those state constitutions in turn often provided a model for later state constitutions. During the Progressive era, when many western states adopted their constitutions, the framers often exhibited profound skepticism about the exercise of government power, and inserted provisions in state constitutions creating the power of voter initiative and recall, and constraints on the creation of monopolies.

State constitutions typically have rich preambles that set the tenor for their interpretation. While the federal constitution did not explicitly incorporate the Declaration of Independence, for instance, no fewer than 35 state constitutions expressly protect the right to life, liberty, and property (or pursuit of happiness). Article I, section 1 of the Alaska Constitution is illustrative of this practice:

> This constitution is dedicated to the principles that all persons have a natural right to life, liberty, and the pursuit of happiness, and the enjoyment of the rewards of their own industry; that all persons are equal and entitled to equal rights, opportunities, and protection under the law; and that all persons have corresponding obligations to the people and to the State.

Likewise, article I, section 1 of the Constitution of the state of Washington states, "All political power is inherent in the people, and governments derive their just powers from the consent of the governed, and are established to protect and maintain individual rights." To make the matter even more pointed, article I, section 32 of the Washington Constitution reminds that "[a] frequent recurrence to fundamental principles is essential to the security of individual rights and the perpetuity of free government." Similar provisions abound in other state constitutions.

At least 15 state constitutions contain protections of equal privileges and immunities. Article I, section 20 of the Oregon Constitution provides, "No law shall be passed granting to any citizen or class of citizens privileges, or immunities, which, upon the same terms, shall not belong to all citizens." State courts are free to—and in many cases do—interpret their own privileges and immunities clauses more generously than the U.S. Supreme Court has interpreted the 14th Amendment privileges or immunities clause. To the same end, at least nine states expressly forbid state-created monopolies. The North Carolina Constitution, which was inspired by John Locke, provides in article I, section 34, "Perpetuities and monopolies are contrary to the genius of a free state and shall not be allowed."

State constitutions restrict governmental powers in other ways. About 40 state constitutions prohibit legislatures from enacting "special" or "local" legislation—in other words, pork-barrel spending. If only such a provision existed in the federal constitution! Properly applied, such provisions prohibit the legislature from including in general budget bills projects that apply only to a given locality or circumstance, instead requiring separate enactment of such legislation. Similarly, at least 41 state constitutions protect the obligation of contracts. No fewer than 14 state constitutions contain express prohibitions against the taking of private property for private use.

How can freedom advocates use such provisions to protect liberty? Ideally, they can take such provisions out of jurisprudential mothballs and invest them with their intended meaning, again using compelling cases to illustrate the concerns about excessive government power that animated the framers.

A good illustration is the Institute for Justice's crusade

against eminent domain abuse. As noted in chapter 5, the U.S. Supreme Court essentially excised the public use limitation on the eminent domain power out of the Fifth Amendment. Hence, federal challenges to the exercise of eminent domain typically are unavailing. So we turned to state constitutions: not only to express provisions limiting the eminent domain power, but to due process principles that ought to constrain government power as well.

To begin the battle, in light of volumes of adverse case precedents, we felt that we needed to find a truly outrageous factual scenario; one with a villain so heinous that a court might feel obliged to constrain local government's rapacious confiscatory appetites. Central casting provided us with precisely the antihero we needed: Donald Trump.

Trump decided that he wanted a parking lot for his limousines adjacent to his casino in Atlantic City. Occupying the property he coveted were a little Italian restaurant named Sabatini's, a gold shop, and a home owned by a feisty lady, Vera Coking. They didn't want to sell. That's fine, said Trump: I'll have Atlantic City use its eminent domain power to take the property. And the city did just that, reasoning that whatever was good for casinos was good for Atlantic City.

Along the way, our litigation campaign had some help. Not only did ABC's John Stossel feature the plight of Vera Coking along with a clip of Donald Trump angrily walking out of his interview, but Garry Trudeau's *Doonesbury* spent an entire week chronicling Trump's greedy efforts (though, with typical artistic license, Trudeau had Trump trying to hire a hit man to knock off the Sabatinis in addition to wielding the power of eminent domain).

In the end, the New Jersey state trial court found that the intended use of the property was private, not public, and it enjoined the city's use of eminent domain. As the *New York*

Times described the victory, "It was a case that pitted a widowed homemaker and the owners of two small businesses against the state and Donald J. Trump, one of the brashest personalities in the casino business. And today, the little guys won."[12]

That precedent, in turn, fueled IJ's efforts in Pennsylvania, Connecticut, New York, Ohio, Arizona, Mississippi, and elsewhere to curb eminent domain abuse. Although state courts are not bound by decisions outside of their own states, they often find decisions in other states persuasive, especially when construing similar constitutional provisions. As a result, it is possible—as IJ's eminent domain abuse efforts illustrate—to conduct a national litigation campaign to advance individual liberty relying on the constitutional protections of the 50 states.

State constitutions can provide an effective safeguard against grassroots tyranny. We have barely tapped their potential. We need badly to start doing so.

Court of Public Opinion

Too often freedom advocates eschew the last of the three venues, assuming that the media are monolithically hostile to freedom. Whatever their politics, the media exhibit one overarching characteristic: skepticism. As the Donald Trump story above illustrates, the media can provide a powerful weapon in the fight for freedom.

At the Institute for Justice, we have worked assiduously to improve the odds in our cases by litigating aggressively in the court of public opinion.* Lawsuits can be important teaching

---

*IJ is enormously lucky to have two consummate communications professionals, John Kramer and Lisa Andaloro Knepper, who choreograph our efforts in the court of public opinion with extraordinary skill and passion.

vehicles. The image of James Meredith walking with federal escorts into the University of Mississippi during the 1950s was probably more significant in expanding freedom than the underlying lawsuit that won him that right. Moreover, media attention can transform cases that lose in the court of law into winners in the real world.

A good example are two economic liberty cases my colleagues and I litigated in the mid-1990s. The first was the case of Taalib-din Uqdah and Pamela Ferrell, two black entrepreneurs who wanted to open an African hairstyling salon in Washington, DC, called Cornrows & Co.[13] Their efforts, which included hiring and training unemployed people, paying taxes, and providing a popular service to consumers in the nation's capital (including many of its politicians), were rewarded by a knock on the door by a District of Columbia police officer bearing an order: Shut down or go to jail. The crime, of course, was braiding hair without the requisite cosmetology license.

The federal judge assigned to the case was sympathetic, and even compared Uqdah and Ferrell's plight to something that might occur in the Soviet Union. (I replied that we were actually thinking of seeking economic asylum for our clients in Russia because these days it seems to value economic liberty more than our own country.) But he ruled against the plaintiffs, finding the weight of case law overwhelmingly against them.

But at the same time, the battle was raging in the court of public opinion. Crusading television reporter John Stossel profiled Uqdah and Ferrell's plight in a segment entitled "Rules, Rules, Stupid Rules." District of Columbia bureaucrats have a high threshold for embarrassment, but Stossel's biting exposé managed to exceed it. While the case was pending on appeal, with the government having won the opening round, the District of Columbia capitulated, and deregulated cosmetology. Today, not only is Cornrows & Co. a thriving business, but dozens of other hair braiding salons operate openly and lawfully, contributing mightily to the economic well-being of our capital city.

In the midst of the hair braiding struggle, my partner Chip Mellor was litigating on behalf of Leroy Jones, who wanted to start a taxicab business in Denver.[14] Jones, who is African American, and three partners who were African immigrants, were driving for the ubiquitous Yellow Cabs. But like many people who work for others, they aspired to go into business for themselves. They realized that there was a huge untapped market in Denver, specifically low-income neighborhoods for which taxicab service was needed but often unavailable. So Jones and his partners set out to start a new co-op company, Quick-Pick Cabs, that would primarily serve low-income areas of Denver and provide better working conditions and benefits for drivers.

Jones and his colleagues had everything they needed: capital, know-how, experience, and a market niche. Everything, that is, except a piece of paper called a "certificate of public convenience or necessity." Jones applied for the certificate, presenting the company's credentials and petitions signed by hundreds of would-be customers. But the Colorado Public Utilities Commission responded with the same decision it had given every applicant for a taxicab license since World War II: application denied. Denver already had three taxicab companies. In order to satisfy the standard of public convenience and necessity, taxicab applicants did not have to show merely that they were qualified and that a market demand existed that the other companies were not adequately serving. They had to demonstrate that the other companies *could not* serve the market—a nearly impossible standard to meet.

So instead of pursuing their share of the American Dream as business owners, Jones and his partners—who by now were fired by Yellow Cab—were forced to toil in lesser employment, such as hawking soft drinks at Mile High Stadium or working in a convenience store.

The Institute for Justice filed a lawsuit on the entrepreneurs' behalf—and lost. Despite compelling and sympathetic facts, the federal district court found that the exacting legal standard could not be met. But the case attracted such visibility in the court of public opinion—editorials in the *Wall Street Journal*, a segment on CBS News "Eye on America," and other outlets—that the state capitulated while the case was on appeal, and deregulated entry into the Denver taxicab market.

While all of that was going on, in the darkest days when it appeared that they would never be able to fulfill their dreams, Jones and his partners realized that their fight was not just about themselves, but part of a bigger battle for economic liberty—the birthright of every American. So they took the symbolic step of changing the name of their company, from Quick-Pick Cabs to Freedom Cabs. And today, a fleet of 50 Freedom Cabs serves customers across Denver. It is therefore fitting to make a brief commercial announcement to the reader: The next time you are in Denver, take a freedom ride in Freedom Cabs.

These cases demonstrate what is possible in the fight against petty tyranny at the local level. The percentage of successful challenges chronicled in this book surely far exceeds the proportion of triumphs against grassroots tyranny in the real world, but I hope they demonstrate that with creativity and perspicacity, victory is possible. As the number and visibility of such victories increase, perhaps state and local government officials will begin to exercise some self-restraint, and so many such battles will no longer be necessary.

Perhaps. But until then we must use every resource at our disposal to protect the American legacy of freedom, and to pass it along to our children in better shape than we found it. That goal is not an easy one. The government has both its own plentiful resources (also known as our tax dollars at work) as well as those of the powerful interests who invariably benefit from grassroots tyranny. The most potent tools we can array in response are the constitutions, federal and state, and the light of day, which exerts the same withering effect on government abuse as sunshine does on a vampire.

But the first step is to get involved. Many of us are involved in national politics, but too few of us are involved at the level at which government affects us most directly—the local level. The threat to freedom is great, to be sure; but when the government takes action that truly affects our lives, that face of government oppression will far more likely belong to a local bureaucrat than to the president. It's remarkable how brazen and unfettered local government has become—especially considering that, at the local level, one person truly can make a difference.

The odds are always against citizen David as he or she battles the governmental Goliath. But my colleagues and I draw inspiration from the words of Thomas Paine, an American revolutionary who persevered against far greater odds than we face today:

> *Tyranny, like hell, is not easily conquered; yet we have this consolation with us, that the harder the conflict, the more glorious the triumph.*[15]

NOTES

Introduction

1. Washington, DC: Cato Institute (1993).

Chapter 1

1. James McGregor Burns, J. W. Peltason, Thomas E. Cronin, and David B. Magleby, *State and Local Politics: Government by the People* (10th ed.) (Upper Saddle River, NJ: Prentice-Hall, 2001), p. 39.
2. Ibid., p. 151.
3. Ibid., p. 6.
4. Michael J. Ross, *State and Local Politics and Policy: Change and Reform* (Englewood Cliffs, NJ: Prentice-Hall, 1987), p. 191.
5. H. V. Savitch and John Clayton Thomas, eds., *Big City Politics in Transition* (Newbury Park, CA: Sage, 1991), pp. 160–61.

6. Burns et al., *State and Local Politics*, p. 6.
7. Virginia Marion Perrenod, *Special Districts, Special Purposes: Fringe Governments and Urban Problems in the Houston Area* (College Station, TX: Texas A&M University Press, 1984), p. 3.
8. David R. Berman, *State and Local Politics* (7th ed.) (Madison, WI: Brown and Benchmark, 1993), p. 216.
9. U.S. Census Bureau, *Statistical Abstract of the United States* (2000), p. 299.
10. Ibid., p. 304.
11. John Maggs, "Sorry States," *National Journal* (Aug. 9, 2003), p. 2537.
12. *Statistical Abstract* (2000), p. 304.
13. U.S. Census Bureau, *State and Local Government Finances by Level of Government and by State* (1999–2000).
14. *Statistical Abstract* (2000), p. 318.
15. Ibid., p. 326.
16. Ibid., p. 301.
17. Louis Uchitelle, "Red Ink in States Beginning to Hurt Economic Recovery," *New York Times* (July 28, 2003), pp. A1 and A10.
18. Gregg Easterbrook, "States' Rites," *New Republic* (Aug. 11, 2003), p. 15.
19. John Maggs, "From Tax Cuts to Tax Hikes," *National Journal* (Aug. 9, 2003), p. 2550.
20. Dennis Cauchon, "Bad Moves, Not Economy, Behind Busted State Budgets," *USA Today* (June 23, 2003), pp. 1A–2A.
21. Easterbrook, "States' Rites," p. 15.
22. Ibid.
23. Ibid., p. 17.
24. Dennis Cauchon, "GOP Outspends Democrats in States," *USA Today* (May 19, 2003), p. 1A.
25. Burns et al., *State and Local Politics*, p. 209.
26. *Statistical Abstract* (2000), p. 445.
27. David Seifman, "Gold Fringe: Benefits Surge Shocks Apple," *New York Post* (May 20, 2003).
28. See Ross, *Politics and Policy*, p. 108.
29. Robert A. Caro, *The Power Broker: Robert Moses and the Fall of New York* (New York: Alfred A. Knopf, 1974), pp. 6–8 and 20.
30. Ibid., pp. 623–24.

31. Ibid., p. 616.
32. Ibid., p. 624.
33. Ibid., pp. 14–15.
34. Ibid., p. 18.
35. Ibid., p. 19.
36. Ibid., p. 632.
37. Ibid., p. 17.
38. Ibid., p. 632.
39. Clay Risen, "Memories of Overdevelopment," *New Republic* (Feb. 23, 2004), p. 26.
40. Ibid.
41. Ibid., pp. 27–28.
42. Paul J. Andrisani, Simon Hakim, and Eva Leeds, eds., *Making Government Work: Lessons from America's Governors and Mayors* (Lanham, MD: Rowman and Littlefield, 2000), p. 14.
43. John C. Bollens, *Special District Governments in the United States* (Westport, CT: Greenwood Press, 1957), p. 1.
44. Nancy Burns, *The Formation of American Local Governments* (New York: Oxford University Press, 1994), p. 12.
45. Ibid., p. 12.
46. Ibid., p. 53.
47. As other types of special districts have grown, the number of school districts has shrunk dramatically—from 108,579 in 1942 to only 13,726 in 1997. See U.S. Census Bureau, *Statistical Abstract of the United States* (2000), p. 299. Ordinarily, a diminution in the number of governments might constitute a favorable development; but here the overwhelming trend is toward consolidation into large school districts that are more responsive to special interest pressures than to the wishes of parents and the needs of children. See John H. Chubb and Terry M. Moe, *Politics, Markets & America's Schools* (Washington, DC: Brookings Institution, 1990).
48. *Statistical Abstract* (2000), p. 299.
49. Bollens, *Special District Governments*, p. 69.
50. Bernard H. Ross, Myron A. Levine, and Murray S. Stedman, *Urban Politics: Power in Metropolitan America* (4th ed.) (Ithaca, NY: F. E. Peacock, 1991), p. 298.
51. Burns, *American Local Governments*, p. 12.
52. Ibid., p. 27.

53. Ross et al., *Urban Politics*, pp. 298–99.

54. Perrenod, *Special Districts*, pp. 41 and 117.

55. Diana B. Henriques, *The Machinery of Greed: Public Authority Abuse and What to Do About It* (Lexington, MA: Lexington Books, 1986). Apart from Caro's biography of Robert Moses, Henriques's book is the finest critique of special authorities I have encountered.

56. Ibid., p. 15.

57. Michael S. Gruen, "Government by Subterfuge," *City Journal* (Winter 1995), reprinted at http://www.city-journal.org/html/5_1_govt_by.html.

58. Ibid.

59. See generally Andrisani et al.

60. Haya El Nasser, "Some Big Places Find Paradise in *Not* Being Real Cities," *USA Today* (June 25, 2003), p. 1A.

61. See www.nlc.org.

62. See http://www.afscme.org/private/index.html.

Chapter 2

1. It is a topic that I treat in greater detail in Clint Bolick, *Grassroots Tyranny: The Limits of Federalism* (Washington, DC: Cato Institute, 1993), pp.13–92.

2. Felix Morley, *Freedom and Federalism* (Indianapolis: Liberty Press ed., 1981), p. xxiv.

3. See Timothy Conlan, *New Federalism* (Washington: Brookings Institution, 1988), p. 3.

4. Daniel J. Elazar, *Exploring Federalism* (Tuscaloosa, AL: University of Alabama Press, 1987), p. 91. Elazar explores in depth the origins and history of federalism. See pp. 115–52.

5. Robert H. Bork, *Federalism and Federal Regulation: The Case of Product Labeling* (Washington, DC: Washington Legal Foundation, 1991), p. 1.

6. A good essay on the tasks confronting the framers and the structural methods they devised to achieve them is Akhil Reed Amar, "Of Sovereignty and Federalism," 96 *Yale Law Journal* 1425, 1439–51 (1987).

7. Edward S. Corwin, "The 'Higher Law' Background of American Constitutional Law," in Randy E. Barnett, ed., *The Rights*

Retained by the People (Fairfax, VA: George Mason University Press, 1989), pp. 83–84.

8. James Madison, "Speech to the House Explaining His Proposed Amendment and His Notes for the Amendment Speech," in Barnett, *The Rights Retained*, p. 61.

9. *The Federalist* No. 10 (Madison), in *The Federalist Papers* (New York: Modern Library, 1937), pp. 60–61. All subsequent *Federalist* citations pertain to this text.

10. See, e.g., David A. Logan, "Judicial Federalism in the Court of History," 66 *Oregon Law Review* 453, 467 n. 68 (1988).

11. *The Federalist* No. 15 (Hamilton), p. 89.

12. John C. Yoo, "The Judicial Safeguards of Federalism," 70 *Southern California Law Review* 1311, 1403 (1997).

13. Quoted in Randy E. Barnett, "James Madison's Ninth Amendment," in Barnett, *The Rights Retained*, p. 21.

14. Quoted in *The Great Debate: Interpreting Our Written Constitution* (Washington: Federalist Society, 1986), p. 16.

15. *The Federalist* No. 10 (Madison), p. 54.

16. Ibid., p. 58.

17. Ibid., pp. 57–58.

18. Morley, *Freedom and Federalism*, p. 31.

19. Amar, "Of Sovereignty and Federalism," p. 1426.

20. Quoted in Raoul Berger, *Federalism: The Founders' Design* (Norman, OK: University of Oklahoma Press, 1987), p. 52.

21. *The Federalist* No. 46 (Madison), p. 305.

22. Ibid., pp. 304–05.

23. *U.S. Term Limits, Inc. v. Thornton*, 514 U.S. 779, 838 (1995) (Kennedy, J., concurring); quoted in *Saenz v. Roe*, 526 U.S. 489, 504 n. 17 (1999).

24. Madison, "Speech to the House," in Barnett, *The Rights Retained*, p. 61.

25. Ibid.

26. Quoted in Morley, *Freedom and Federalism*, p. 27.

27. Bork, *Federalism and Federal Regulation*, p. 4.

28. *The Federalist* No. 44 (Madison), p. 291.

29. Quoted in Berger, *Federalism*, p. 63.

30. *The Federalist* No. 51 (Hamilton or Madison), pp. 338–39.

31. *The Federalist* No. 46 (Madison), p. 306.

32. Quoted in Logan, "Judicial Federalism," p. 467.

33. Barnett, in Barnett, *The Rights Retained*, p. 34.

34. Ibid., p. 41.

35. Ronald D. Rotunda, "The New States' Rights, the New Federalism, the New Commerce Clause, and the Proposed New Abdication," 25 *Oklahoma City Law Review* 869, 869–70 (2000).

36. Barnett, in Barnett, *The Rights Retained*, p. 41.

37. 32 U.S. 243, 250 (1833).

38. Robert J. Harris, "States' Rights and Vested Interests," in Gary L. McDowell, ed., *Taking the Constitution Seriously* (Dubuque, IA: Kendall/Hunt, 1981), p. 179.

39. *Dred Scott v. Sandford*, 19 How. 399, 410 (60 U.S. 663) (1857).

40. Michael Kent Curtis, *No State Shall Abridge* (Durham, NC: Duke University Press, 1986), pp. 30–31. See also Clint Bolick, *Changing Course: Civil Rights at the Crossroads* (New Brunswick, NJ: Transaction Books, 1988), pp. 19–21.

41. Harold M. Hyman, "Federalism: Legal Fiction and Historical Artifact?" 15 *Brigham Young Law Review* 905, 919 (1987).

42. J. M. Balkin, "Federalism and the Conservative Ideology," 19 *Urban Lawyer* 473 (1987).

43. Ibid.

44. Curtis, *No State Shall Abridge*, p. 41.

45. Quoted in Alfred Avins, ed., *The Reconstruction Amendments' Debates* (Wilmington, DE: Delaware Law School, 1974), p. 136.

46. Quoted in Clint Bolick, *Unfinished Business: A Civil Rights Strategy for America's Third Century* (San Francisco: Pacific Research Institute, 1990), p. 26.

Chapter 3

1. For an account of the intended scope of the privileges or immunities clause and its subsequent evisceration, see Bolick, *Unfinished Business*, pp. 47–91.

2. *Slaughter-House Cases*, 83 U.S. 36, 96 (1873) (Field, J., dissenting).

3. Ibid. at 110 (Field, J., dissenting).

4. 163 U.S. 537 (1896).

5. For a superb account of that case and its origins in the jurisprudence of *Slaughter-House*, see Charles A. Lofgren, *The Plessy Case* (New York: Oxford University Press, 1987).

6. 347 U.S. 483 (1954).

7. See, e.g., *Lochner v. New York*, 198 U.S. 45 (1905).

8. See, e.g., *Pierce v. Society of Sisters*, 268 U.S. 510 (1925). Unlike other substantive due process cases from that period, the *Pierce* line of cases remains good law today.

9. See, e.g., *West Coast Hotel Co. v. Parrish*, 300 U.S. 379 (1937). This phenomenon is recounted in Steven M. Simpson, "Judicial Abdication and the Rise of Special Interests," 6 *Chapman Law Review* 173, 177 (2003).

10. See Curtis, *No State Shall Abridge*, p. 203 (see ch. 2, n. 40). For a discussion of the origins of the dichotomy between fundamental and nonfundamental rights, see Simpson, "Judicial Abdication," p. 184.

11. See, e.g., *Nollan v. California Coastal Commission*, 483 U.S. 825 (1987). For a masterful treatment of how the takings clause should be used to constrain government power, see Richard A. Epstein, *Takings* (Cambridge, MA: Harvard University Press, 1985).

12. I always get nervous any time an adjective is used before the term "justice." Regardless of the adjective employed, it typically tends to serve as a nullification or distortion of ordinary concepts of justice.

13. That is not to say that the Warren Court was entirely misguided. Its deployment of the equal protection clause to strike down segregated education; its recognition of a general right to privacy, however awkwardly conceived; and its strong protections of freedom of speech all helped to vindicate the framers' intent of a judicial bulwark against governmental tyranny.

14. *United States v. Darby*, 312 U.S. 100, 124 (1940).

15. Robert H. Freilich, "A Proposed Congressional 'Statute of Federalism'," 19 *Urban Lawyer* 539, 541–42 (1987).

16. 285 U.S. 262, 311 (1932) (Brandeis, J., dissenting).

17. Ibid., p. 280 (majority).

18. William J. Brennan, Jr., "Some Aspects of Federalism," 39 *New York University Law Review* 945, 959 (1964).

19. For an insightful examination of Brennan's shifting views, see Earl M. Maltz, "False Prophet—Justice Brennan and the Theory of State Constitutional Law," 15 *Hastings Constitutional Law Quarterly* 429, 430 (1988).

20. William J. Brennan, Jr., "State Constitutions and the Protection of Individual Rights," 90 *Harvard Law Review* 489, 502 (1977).

See also Jon O. Newman, "The 'Old Federalism': Protection of Individual Rights by State Constitutions in an Era of Federal Passivity," 15 *Connecticut Law Review* 21 (1982–83).

21. Brennan, "State Constitutions," p. 491.

22. Quoted in William Bennett Turner and Beth S. Brinkman, "The Constitution of First Resort," *California Lawyer* (June 1989), p. 52.

23. Brennan, speech delivered at Georgetown University (1985), in *The Great Debate: Interpreting Our Written Constitution* (Washington, DC: Federalist Society, 1986), p. 16.

24. *San Antonio Independent School District v. Rodriguez*, 411 U.S. 1 (1973).

25. See, e.g., *Serrano v. Priest*, 487 P.2d 1241 (Cal. 1971); *Robinson v. Cahill*, 303 A.2d 273 (N.J. 1973).

26. *Lloyd Corp. v. Tanner*, 407 U.S. 551 (1972).

27. Brennan, "State Constitutions," p. 496.

28. *Robins v. PruneYard Shopping Center*, 23 C.3d 899 (1979).

29. *PruneYard Shopping Center v. Robins*, 447 U.S. 79, 81–83 (1980).

30. Ibid. at 91 (Marshall, J., concurring).

31. Raoul Berger, *Federalism: The Founders' Design* (Norman, OK: University of Oklahoma Press, 1987), p. 52.

32. Stephen Macedo, *The New Right v. the Constitution* (Washington, DC: Cato Institute, 1987), p. 25.

33. Robert H. Bork, *The Tempting of America* (New York: Free Press, 1990), pp. 184–85.

34. Quoted in Randy E. Barnett, ed., *The Rights Retained by the People* (Fairfax, VA: George Mason University Press, 1989), p. 1.

35. Calvin R. Massey, "Federalism and Fundamental Rights: The Ninth Amendment," 38 *Hastings Law Journal* 305, 316–17 (1987).

36. See, e.g., Berger, *Federalism*, p. 26. Here, Berger explicitly rejects the statement made by Justice Joseph Story that the union "was emphatically the act of the whole people of the united colonies."

37. Bork, *The Tempting of America*, pp. 52–53.

38. Raoul Berger, "The Ninth Amendment," in Barnett, *The Rights Retained*, p. 218.

39. Robert H. Bork, *Tradition and Morality in Constitutional Law* (Washington, DC: American Enterprise Institute, 1984), pp. 8–9.

40. Bork, *The Tempting of America*, p. 119.

41. Amar, "Of Sovereignty and Federalism," p. 1520 (see ch. 2, n. 6).

42. Michael S. Greve, "Federalism's Frontier," 7 *Texas Review of Law & Politics* 93, 126 (2002).

43. 426 U.S. 833 (1976).

44. 469 U.S. 528 (1985).

45. *National League of Cities*, 426 U.S. at 845.

46. Ibid. at 858 (Brennan, J., dissenting).

47. Ibid. at 859 (Brennan, J., dissenting).

48. *Garcia*, 469 U.S. at 556.

49. Ibid. at 560 (Powell, J., dissenting).

50. Ibid. at 570 (Powell, J., dissenting).

51. Ibid. at 571 (Powell, J., dissenting).

52. Ibid. at 572 (Powell, J., dissenting) (emphasis added).

53. Ibid. at 567 (Powell, J., dissenting).

54. Ibid. at 580 (Rehnquist, J., dissenting).

55. See generally Yoo, "The Judicial Safeguards of Federalism" (see ch. 2, n. 12).

56. See Rotunda, "The New States' Rights," pp. 911–24 (see ch. 2, n. 35). For differing perspectives on the impact of those cases, see Calvin R. Massey, "The Tao of Federalism," 20 *Harvard Journal of Law & Public Policy* 887, 899–903 (1997); and Vicki C. Jackson, "Narratives of Federalism: Of Continuities and Comparative Constitutional Experience," 51 *Duke Law Journal* 223 (2001).

57. 514 U.S. 549 (1995).

58. 529 U.S. 598 (2000).

59. *Lopez*, 514 U.S. at 552.

60. *Lopez*, 514 U.S. at 559; *Morrison*, 529 U.S. at 609–11.

61. In *Employment Division, Department of Human Resources of Oregon v. Smith*, 494 U.S. 872 (1990), the Court retreated from its previous free exercise of jurisprudence by upholding a law that denied Native Americans the right to use peyote during religious ceremonies.

62. 521 U.S. 507 (1997).

63. *City of Boerne*, 521 U.S. 519–29.

64. 505 U.S. 144 (1992).

65. *New York*, 505 U.S. at 177.

66. *New York*, 505 U.S. at 161.

67. *Printz v. United States*, 521 U.S. 898 (1997).

68. *City of Lafayette v. Louisiana Power & Light Co.*, 435 U.S. 389, 439 (1978); *Community Communications Co. v. City of Boulder*, 455 U.S. 40 (1982).

69. *City of Lafayette*, 435 U.S. at 439 (1978) (Stewart, J., dissenting).

70. Ibid. at 408 (majority).

71. For a depiction of the internal battle within the Reagan administration, see Bolick, *Grassroots Tyranny*, pp. 87–88 (see ch. 2, n. 1).

72. Justice Kennedy was joined by Justices Stevens, O'Connor, Souter, Ginsburg, and Breyer.

73. *Romer v. Evans*, 517 U.S. 620, 627 (1996).

74. Ibid. at 630.

75. Ibid. at 623.

76. Ibid. at 635.

77. Ibid. at 636 (Scalia, J., dissenting).

78. Ibid. at 653 (Scalia, J., dissenting).

79. Ibid. at 652 (Scalia, J., dissenting).

80. This constitutional prognosticator, drawing from the justices' positions in previous decisions including *Romer*, confidently predicted that not a single justice would vote to accept review in *Bush v. Gore*. The liberals would not do so because they would not want to disturb prospects for a Democratic victory, I reasoned, while conservatives would refrain from doing so due to their deeply held convictions on federalism. I was wrong.

81. *Bush v. Gore*, 531 U.S. 98, 104 (2000). A concurring opinion by Chief Justice Rehnquist joined by Justices Scalia and Thomas based the decision on stronger jurisprudential ground, specifically the constitutional role delegated in the presidential election context to state legislatures. Ibid. at 111 (Rehnquist, C.J., concurring).

82. Ibid. at 111 (Rehnquist, C.J., concurring).

83. Ibid. at 112 (Rehnquist, C.J., concurring).

84. Ibid. at 110 (majority). At least when conservatives engage in judicial activism, they hang a sign on it saying, "Good for today only": Ibid. ("Our consideration is limited to the present circumstances").

85. Ibid. at 128 (Stevens, J., dissenting).

86. Ibid. at 141 (Ginsburg, J., dissenting).
87. Ibid. at 142 (Ginsburg, J., dissenting).
88. Amar, "Of Sovereignty and Federalism," p. 1520 (see ch. 2, n. 6).
89. Cass R. Sunstein, "Federal Appeal," *New Republic* (Dec. 22, 2003), p. 23.

Chapter 4

1. *Chaddock v. Day*, 42 N.W. 977, 978 (Mich. 1889).
2. For a description of the California hair braiding controversy, see, e.g., Karen E. Klein, "What it Takes to Take On the State Regulators," *Los Angeles Times* (Nov. 3, 1999); "Hair Raising," *Wall Street Journal* (Sept. 1, 1999).
3. *Cornwell v. Hamilton*, 80 F.Supp.2d 1101 (S.D. Cal. 1999).
4. So far we have completed studies of barriers to entrepreneurship in Washington State, Arizona, Baltimore, Boston, Charlotte, Detroit, New York City, San Antonio, and San Diego. See http://ij.org/publications/index.html.
5. See S. David Young, *The Rule of Experts: Occupational Licensing in America* (Washington, DC: Cato Institute, 1987).
6. Walter Williams, *The State Against Blacks* (New York: McGraw-Hill, 1982), p. xvi.
7. For a good account of abuses of economic liberty, see Randy Fitzgerald, *Mugged by the State: Outrageous Government Assaults on Ordinary People and Their Property* (Washington, DC: Regnery Publishing, 2003), pp. 109–26. For additional examples, see Bolick, *Grassroots Tyranny*, pp. 141–52 (see ch. 2, n. 1).
8. See, e.g., *New Orleans v. Dukes*, 427 U.S. 297 (1976). For a fuller discussion of the erosion of protection for economic liberty, see Bolick, *Unfinished Business*, pp. 47–91 (see ch. 2, n. 46).
9. *Federal Communications Commission v. Beach Communications*, 508 U.S. 307 (1993).
10. Anthony Ramirez, "Judge Rejects Most of Law on Commuter Van Licenses," *New York Times* (Mar. 24, 1999).
11. Richard N. Velotta, "Independent Limo Operators Fight Rule," *Las Vegas Sun* (May 4, 1998).
12. "A Win for the Little Guy," *Las Vegas Review-Journal* (May 18, 2001).

13. *Craigmiles v. Giles*, 110 F.Supp.2d 658 (E.D. Tenn. 2000); see also Ronnie Moore, "Casket Stores Win Right to Sell Without License," *Chattanooga Free Press* (Aug. 22, 2000); "Economic Liberty Alive and Well," *Chattanooga Free Press* (Sept. 13, 2000).

14. *Craigmiles v. Giles*, 312 F.3d 220 (6th Cir. 2002).

15. *Powers v. Harris*, 2002 U.S. Dist. LEXIS 26939 (Dec. 12, 2002).

16. Chi-Dooh Li, "What Is the City Council Thinking?" *Seattle Post-Intelligencer* (Sept. 25, 2003).

17. Benjamin Minnick, "City Rule Has Haulers Talkin' Trash," *Seattle Daily Journal of Commerce* (May 14, 2003), p. 1.

18. William R. Mauer, "Waste Monopoly Trashes Free Market," *Seattle Post-Intelligencer* (May 16, 2003).

19. Lisa Heyamoto, "Small Firm Sues City Over Hauling Rules," *Seattle Times* (May 14, 2003).

20. Federal Trade Commission, *Possible Anticompetitive Barriers to E-Commerce: Wine* (July 2003), available at http:www.ftc.gov/os/2003/07/winereport2.pdf.

21. Compare *Heald v. Engler*, 342 F.3d 517 (6th Cir. 2003); *Dickerson v. Bailey*, 336 F.3d 388 (5th Cir. 2003); *Beskind v. Easley*, 325 F.3d 506 (4th Cir. 2003); and *Bolick v. Roberts*, 199 F.Supp.2d 397 (E.D. Va. 2002), *vacated and remanded sub. nom. Bolick v. Daniel-son*, 330 F.3d 274 (4th Cir. 2003); with *Swedenburg v. Kelly*, 2004 U.S. App. LEXIS 52337 (Feb. 12, 2004); and *Bridenbaugh v. Freeman-Wilson*, 227 F.3d 848 (7th Cir. 2000).

22. "Rats! Bureaucrats' Bullying of an Enterprising Teenager Is Shameful," *East Valley Tribune* (Mar. 16, 2004), p. 29. See also Cindy Hernandez, "Lessons Learned After School," *Arizona Republic* (Apr. 7, 2004).

23. Quoted in "The Vans Roll," *Wall Street Journal* (Aug. 13, 1997).

Chapter 5

1. Elisabeth Rosenthal, "Factories Wrest Land from China's Farmers," *New York Times* (March 23, 2003), p. A10.

2. For additional examples, see Fitzgerald, *Mugged by the State*, pp. 21–34 (see ch. 4, n. 7). Other accounts of violations of private-property rights are described in Bolick, *Grassroots Tyranny*, pp. 111–22 (see ch. 2, n. 1).

3. *Bailey v. Myers*, 76 P.3d 898 (Ariz. App. 2003).

4. Dana Berliner, *Public Power, Private Gain* (Washington, DC: Institute for Justice, 2003). The report can be found at http://

www.castlecoalition.org/report/. Because the number of cases it can handle is limited, while the number of abuses is enormous, the Institute for Justice launched the Castle Coalition to provide tools to help grassroots activists combat eminent domain abuse.

5. Ibid., p. 2.
6. Ibid., pp. 144–54.
7. 467 U.S. 229 (1984).
8. Berliner, *Public Power, Private Gain*, pp. 115–16.
9. See Blaine Harden, "In Ohio, a Test for Eminent Domain," *Washington Post* (June 22, 2003), p. A3.
10. Transcript, *60 Minutes*, CBS (Sept. 28, 2003).
11. The bible for property-rights advocates in fighting government's power to take property is the brilliant classic by Richard A. Epstein, *Takings: Private Property and the Power of Eminent Domain* (Cambridge, MA: Harvard University Press, 1985).
12. *Pennsylvania Coal Co. v. Mahon*, 260 U.S. 393, 415 (1922).
13. See Bolick, *Grassroots Tyranny*, pp. 113–14 (see ch. 2, n. 1); Marcia Coyle, "Property Revival," *National Law Journal* (January 27, 1992).
14. *Lucas v. South Carolina Coastal Council*, 505 U.S. 1003 (1992).
15. The Court's recent decision in *Tahoe-Sierra Preservation Council, Inc. v. Tahoe Regional Planning Agency*, 535 U.S. 302 (2002), holding that a lengthy development moratorium did not on its face amount to a compensable temporary taking, illustrates the conundrum that property owners face.
16. *Dolan v. City of Tigard*, 512 U.S. 374, 386–392 (1994).
17. In 2000, President Clinton signed into law a bill sponsored by Rep. Henry Hyde raising the burden of proof in federal civil-asset forfeiture proceedings and implementing other reforms. But the legislation did not alter oppressive state rules.
18. *Bennis v. Michigan*, 516 U.S. 442 (1996).
19. Jim Edwards, "Prosecutors React to Knockdown Forfeiture Spending," *New Jersey Law Journal* (Dec. 20, 2002).
20. *State of New Jersey v. One 1990 Ford Thunderbird*, letter opinion, No. CUM-L-000720-99 N.J. Super. Ct., Dec. 11, 2002), at 8.
21. Tanya Kornelsen, "Court Axes Inspection Policy," *Matteson/Richton Park (IL) Star* (March 8, 1998).
22. *Black v. Village of Park Forest*, 20 F.Supp.2d 1218 (N.D. Ill. 1998).
23. *U.S. v. Carolene Products*, 304 U.S. 144, 152 n.4 (1938).

24. *Dolan*, 512 U.S. at 512.
25. *U.S. v. James Daniel Good Real Property*, 510 U.S. 43, 61 (1993).

Chapter 6

1. See Susan Finch, "Couple Win One for the Books," *New Orleans Times-Picayune* (June 18, 2003).
2. *Wexler v. City of New Orleans*, 267 F.Supp.2d 559, 568 (E.D. La. 2003).
3. Examples of the abuse of free-speech rights by state and local governments are set forth in Bolick, *Grassroots Tyranny*, pp. 123–40 (see ch. 2, n. 1).
4. See Jason Emerson, "Doughnut Shop Sues Mesa," *East Valley Tribune* (Jan. 9, 2003); Court Rich, "Mesa Takes Strong Stand on Weak Law," *Arizona Republic* (Jan. 11, 2003). Court Rich is ably litigating the case pro bono with the Institute for Justice Arizona Chapter.
5. See Gordy Holt, "Bagel Business Sues Redmond Over Sign Ban," *Seattle Post-Intelligencer* (July 24, 2003); Nick Perry, "Group Bankrolls Suit on Behalf of Bagel Shop," *The Seattle Times* (July 24, 2003); Christine Frey, "Blazing Bagels Fights Redmond's Sign Rules," *Seattle Post-Intelligencer* (July 27, 2003).
6. *Ballen v. City of Redmond*, slip op., No. C03-2580Z (W.D. Wash. Jan. 21, 2004) at 9.
7. "Just Sue It: Supreme Court Skips Nike, Consumer Speech Dispute," *Palm Beach Daily Business Review* (June 27, 2003).
8. *Kasky v. Nike, Inc.*, 45 P.3d 243 (Ca. 2002).
9. Ibid. at 268 (Brown, J., dissenting, citing Kozinski and Banner, "Who's Afraid of Commercial Speech?" 76 *Virginia Law Review* 627, 627 (1990)). Alex Kozinski, the co-author of the cited article, is a judge on the U.S. Court of Appeals for the Ninth Circuit and a leading critic of the commercial speech doctrine.
10. Ibid. at 268 (Brown, J., dissenting) (emphasis in original).
11. Ibid. at 280 (Brown, J., dissenting) (emphasis in original).
12. *Nike, Inc. v. Kasky*, 123 S.Ct. 2554 (2003).
13. Christopher Schurtz, "Campaign Signs Must Go," *Las Cruces Sun-News* (Jan. 3, 2004).
14. This system accounted for State Attorney General Janet Napolitano's narrow victory in the 2002 gubernatorial race. Ms. Napolitano's campaign coffers were filled with public subsidies, while her opponent, former U.S. Representative Matt Salmon,

refused to accept them. See Clint Bolick, "Fundraising Arizona," *Weekly Standard* (Dec. 2, 2002).

15. Daniel Burnette, "Lobbyist Fee Unconstitutional, Court Surcharge OK Superior Court Judge Rules on Clean Elections Act Funding," *Arizona Capitol Times* (Dec. 31, 2002).

16. *May v. McNally*, 55 P.3d 768 (2002).

Chapter 7

1. Additional examples of abuses of privacy rights are depicted in Bolick, *Grassroots Tyranny*, pp. 153–62 (see ch. 2, n. 1).

2. An excellent case for protecting the right to privacy under the Ninth Amendment is made in Calvin R. Massey, "Federalism and Fundamental Rights: The Ninth Amendment," 38 *Hastings Law Journal* 305 (1987).

3. See Clint Bolick, "Flip-Flopping on Free Association," *Washington Post* (June 17, 2003), p. A21.

4. *Lawrence v. Texas*, 123 S.Ct. 2472, 2476–77 (2003).

5. 478 U.S. 186, 190 (1986).

6. *Lawrence*, 123 S.Ct. at 2475.

7. Ibid. at 2478.

8. Ibid. at 2480.

9. *Planned Parenthood of Southeastern Pennsylvania v. Casey*, 505 U.S. 833, 847 (1992); quoted in *Lawrence*, 123 S.Ct. at 2484.

10. *Lawrence*, 123 S.Ct. at 2497 (Scalia, J., dissenting).

11. Ibid. at 2498 (Scalia, J., dissenting).

12. Ibid. at 2497 (Scalia, J., dissenting).

13. Ibid. at 2498 (Thomas, J., dissenting).

14. *Boy Scouts of America v. Dale*, 530 U.S. 640, 645 (2000) (internal quote marks omitted).

15. Ibid. at 646.

16. Ibid. at 647–48 (quoting *Roberts v. United States Jaycees*, 468 U.S. 609, 622–23 (1984)).

17. Ibid. at 661.

18. Ibid. at 664 (Stevens, J., dissenting).

19. Ibid. at 678.

Chapter 8

1. Sue Ann Pressley, "Texas Interracial Adoption Case Reflects National Debate," *Washington Post* (Jan. 2, 1997).

2. Steven A. Holmes, "Bitter Racial Dispute Rages Over Adoption," *New York Times* (Apr. 13, 1995) (emphasis added).

3. Ibid.

4. Pressley, "Texas Interracial Adoption Case."

5. Holmes, "Bitter Racial Dispute."

6. Ibid.

7. Steven A. Holmes, "Texas Approves Couple's Adoption of 2 Black Boys," *New York Times* (Apr. 15, 1995).

8. The nondiscrimination provisions regarding adoption placements are now codified at 42 U.S.C. 5115a.

9. 347 U.S. 483 (1954).

10. Other examples of government-imposed racial classifications are described in Bolick, *Grassroots Tyranny*, pp. 163–74 (see ch. 2, n. 1).

11. Quoted in Gerald Sorin, *Abolitionism: A New Perspective* (New York: Praeger, 1972), p. 31 (emphasis omitted).

12. See Bolick, *Unfinished Business* (see ch. 2, n. 46).

13. *Korematsu v. United States*, 323 U.S. 214, 245–36 (1944) (Jackson, J., dissenting).

14. The history of the quest for equality under the law in America, and the many departures from that principle, are described in Clint Bolick, *The Affirmative Action Fraud: Can We Restore the American Civil Rights Vision?* (Washington, DC: Cato Institute, (1996)); and Bolick, *Changing Course* (see ch. 2, n. 40).

15. See, e.g., Maria Puente, "Asians, Whites Join Forces in School Integration Debate," *USA Today* (Sept. 11, 1995).

16. Sam Howe Verhovek, "Americans Reject Means But Not Ends of Racial Diversity," *New York Times* (Dec. 14, 1997), sec. 1, p. 1.

17. See Stuart Taylor Jr., "Do African-Americans Really Want Racial Preferences?" *National Journal* (Dec. 20, 2002).

18. *Dea v. Washington Suburban Sanitary Comm'n*, unpublished opinion, No. 97–1572 (4th Cir. June 15, 2001). See "Engineer Who Refused to Comply With Policy Protected under Title VII Opposition Clause," *Daily Labor Report* (June 26, 2001).

19. See, e.g., *Wygant v. Jackson Board of Education*, 476 U.S. 267 (1986); *City of Richmond v. J.A. Croson Co.*, 488 U.S. 469 (1989); *Adarand Constructors, Inc. v. Pena*, 515 U.S. 200 (1995).

20. *Regents of the University of California v. Bakke*, 438 U.S. 265 (1978).

21. Stephan Thernstrom and Abigail Thernstrom, *America in Black*

and White: One Nation, Indivisible (New York: Simon & Schuster, 1999), pp. 357 and 397.

22. Jay P. Greene and Greg Forster, "College Diversity: Fix the Pipeline First," *Washington Post* (Jan. 7, 2004), p. A21.

23. See, e.g., William Julius Wilson, *The Truly Disadvantaged: The Inner City, the Underclass, and Public Policy* (Chicago: University of Chicago Press, 1990); Bolick, *The Affirmative Action Fraud*.

24. Michael Scott Moore, "Affirmative Reaction," *SF Weekly* (Nov. 12, 1997).

25. James Traub, "The Class of Prop. 209," *New York Times* (May 2, 1999), sec. 6, p. 44.

26. Jim Yardley, "Desperately Seeking Diversity," *New York Times* (Apr. 14, 2002), sec. 4A, p. 28; "Governor's One Florida Plan Works," *Fort Myers (FL) News-Press* (June 21, 2002), p. 8B.

27. The Court's opinion was authored by Chief Justice William Rehnquist. Joining Rehnquist in striking down the undergraduate preferences were Justices Sandra Day O'Connor, Antonin Scalia, Anthony Kennedy, Clarence Thomas, and Stephen Breyer. Dissenting were Justices John Paul Stevens, David Souter, and Ruth Bader Ginsburg.

28. *Gratz v. Bollinger*, 539 U.S. 244, 271 (2003).

29. Ibid. at 285 (O'Connor, J., concurring).

30. *Grutter v. Bollinger*, 539 U.S. 306, 324 (2003). Justice O'Connor authored the Court's opinion. Joining O'Connor in the majority were Justices Stevens, Souter, Ginsburg, and Breyer.

31. Ibid. at 327.

32. Ibid. at 332.

33. Ibid. at 336.

34. Dissenting were Chief Justice Rehnquist and Justices Scalia, Kennedy, and Thomas.

35. *Grutter*, 539 U.S. at 371 (Kennedy, J., dissenting).

36. Ibid.

37. Ibid. at 363 (Thomas, J., concurring in part and dissenting in part).

38. Ibid. at 360 (Thomas, J., concurring in part and dissenting in part).

39. Ibid. at 349 n.3 (Thomas, J., concurring in part and dissenting in part).

40. Ibid. at 349 (Thomas, J., concurring in part and dissenting in part).

41. Ibid. at 341.

42. Ibid. at 342.

43. Ibid. at 359 (Thomas, J., concurring in part and dissenting in part).

44. Dan Beyers, "Diversity's Double Bind: Montgomery, Citing Race Policy, Won't Let Girls Switch Schools," *Washington Post* (Aug. 22, 1995), p. A1.

45. Dan Beyers, "Montgomery Reverses Itself, Lets Asian Girls Switch Schools," *Washington Post* (Sept. 14, 1995), p. A1.

Chapter 9

1. *Herndon by Herndon v. Chapel Hill–Carrboro City Board of Education*, 89 F.3d 174 (4th Cir. 1997); *Immediato v. Rye Neck School District*, 73 F.3d 454 (2d Cir. 1996); see also Michael Winerip, "Required Volunteerism: School Programs Tested," *New York Times* (Sept. 23, 1996), p. A16.

2. My account of the first 12 years of the battle to defend school choice programs is Clint Bolick, *Voucher Wars: Waging the Legal Battle Over School Choice* (Washington, DC: Cato Institute, 2003).

3. *Zelman v. Simmons-Harris*, 536 U.S. 639 (2002).

4. Abigail Thernstrom and Stephan Thernstrom, *No Excuses: Closing the Racial Gap in Learning* (New York: Simon & Schuster, 2003).

5. Thernstrom and Thernstrom, *No Excuses*, p. 274.

6. The plight of inner-city schoolchildren, as well as policy prescriptions to redress it, are set forth in Clint Bolick, *Transformation: The Promise and Politics of Empowerment* (Oakland, CA: Institute for Contemporary Studies, 1998), pp. 34–67.

7. National Center for Education Statistics, *The Nation's Report Card: Fourth Grade Reading 2000*, p. 33.

8. Michael Dobbs, "At Colleges, An Affirmative Reaction," *Washington Post* (Nov. 15, 2003), p. A11.

9. Jay P. Green and Marcus A. Winters, *Public School Graduation Rates in the United States* (New York: Manhattan Institute, 2002), p. 3.

10. *Pierce v. Society of Sisters*, 268 U.S. 510, 534–35 (1925). See also *Meyer v. Nebraska*, 262 U.S. 390 (1923) (striking down law forbidding instruction in German as violating parental liberty); *Far-*

rington v. Tokushige, 273 U.S. 284 (1927) (invalidating pervasive regulation of Japanese schools). All three decisions remain good law today.

11. John E. Chubb and Terry M. Moe, *Politics, Markets & America's Schools* (Washington, DC: Brookings Institution, 1990).

12. Ibid., p. 140.

13. Ibid., pp. 215–29. See also Bolick, *Transformation*, pp. 62–67.

14. Chubb and Moe, *America's Schools*, p. 227.

15. Ibid., p. 229.

16. See Bolick, *Transformation*, pp. 53–61.

17. See Bolick, *Voucher Wars*, pp. 201–02.

18. Quoted in Bolick, *Transformation*, p. 34.

19. The early struggle for the Milwaukee Parental Choice Program is eloquently chronicled in Mikel Holt, *Not Yet "Free at Last": The Unfinished Business of the Civil Rights Movement* (Oakland, CA: Institute for Contemporary Studies, 2000); and Daniel McGroarty, *Break These Chains: The Battle for School Choice* (Rocklin, CA: Prima Publishing, 1996). See also Bolick, *Voucher Wars*, pp. 15–43.

20. *Davis v. Grover*, 480 N.W.2d 460, 477 (Ceci, J., concurring).

21. See Bolick, *Voucher Wars*.

22. *Zelman*, 536 U.S. at 677 (Thomas, J., concurring).

23. Ibid. at 682 (Thomas, J., concurring).

Chapter 10

1. *The Federalist* No. 48 (Madison), p. 322.

2. See Steven M. Simpson, "Judicial Abdication and the Rise of Special Interests," 6 *Chapman Law Review* 173, 183 (2003).

3. Ibid., pp. 183–84.

4. Ibid., p. 205.

5. IJ's economic liberty litigation strategy was first sketched out in Bolick, *Unfinished Business*, pp. 47–91 (see ch. 2, n. 46).

6. See, e.g., *City of Cleburne v. Cleburne Living Center*, 473 U.S. 432 (1985) (striking down a zoning law that forbade a home for the mentally retarded). A more recent example is *Romer v. Evans*, 517 U.S. 620 (1996) (striking down Colorado's prohibition against local laws forbidding discrimination against homosexuals).

7. *Brown v. Barry*, 710 F. Supp. 352, 355–56 (D.D.C. 1989) (emphasis deleted).

8. *Santos v. City of Houston*, 852 F. Supp. 601, 608 (S.D. Tex. 1994).

9. *Cornwell v. Hamilton*, 80 F.Supp.2d 1101 (S.D. Cal. 1999).

10. *Craigmiles v. Giles*, 110 F.Supp.2d 658 (E.D. Tenn. 2000).

11. See, e.g., *Serrano v. Priest*, 487 P.2d 1241 (Cal. 1971).

12. David M. Herszenhorn, "Widowed Homeowner Foils Trump Bid in Atlantic City," *New York Times* (July 21, 1998).

13. See Bolick, *Grassroots Tyranny*, pp. 141–44 (see ch. 2, n. 1).

14. See Bolick, *Transformation*, pp. 76–80 (see ch. 9, n. 6).

15. Thomas Paine, *The Crisis* (Dec. 23, 1776).

ABOUT THE AUTHOR

Clint Bolick is president of and general counsel for the Alliance for School Choice, the nation's foremost organization advocating school choice programs for economically and otherwise disadvantaged schoolchildren.

Bolick cofounded the Institute for Justice, a public-interest law firm based in Washington, DC, that litigates in support of economic liberty, private-property rights, school choice, and freedom of speech. During his nearly 13 years at IJ, Bolick engaged in cutting-edge constitutional litigation in a variety of areas, including the defense of school choice programs nationwide that culminated in 2002 with the landmark U.S. Supreme Court decision in *Zelman v. Simmons-Harris*. It was also in 2002 that *American Lawyer* named Bolick one of the nation's three lawyers of the year.

Bolick serves as a research fellow with the Hoover Institution. His most recent previous book is *Voucher Wars: Waging the Legal Battle Over School Choice* (Cato Institute, 2003). He has been widely published in such media as the *Wall Street Journal*, the *New York Times*, and the *Washington Post*.

Bolick lives in Phoenix, Arizona, with his wife, Shawnna, and son, Ryne.

INDEX

Leviathan: The Growth of Local
Government and the Erosion of Liberty

"Local governments: Close to the people, laboratories of democracy, disciplined by the taxpayers' right to move. These truisms no longer tell the truth. Bolick explains . . . why [conservatives'] long-held belief in states' rights and local control makes little sense when special interests and judicial activism have acquired more clout in the byways than on the main thoroughfares of American politics. Powerful insights, convincingly presented."

Paul E. Peterson
Shattuck Professor of Government
Harvard University

"In a nation dedicated to secure what the Constitution refers to as the 'blessings of liberty,' a fundamental obligation of lawyers is to protect individual freedom. Few lawyers in this nation surpass Clint Bolick's accomplishments in this respect. In this book, Bolick relates his many fights against oppression as litigation director of the Institute for Justice. He has applied legal concepts and utilized public opinion to secure protections for individual liberties ranging from entrepreneurial freedom to racial justice and property rights. Bolick's story mitigates for me the pain I suffer when I read about lawyers' misdeeds. Bolick also delivers an excellent critique of the enormous and unchecked powers wielded by a leviathan, his apt description for the combined authority of state and local government."

Bernard H. Siegan
Professor of Law
University of San Diego